# TABE®
# SKILL PRACTICE

Test of Adult Basic Education
Practice Test Questions

Copyright © 2014 by Complete Test Preparation Inc. ALL RIGHTS RESERVED. No part of this book may be reproduced or transferred in any form or by any means, graphic, electronic, or mechanical, including photocopying, recording, web distribution, taping, or by any information storage retrieval system, without the written permission of the author.

Notice: Complete Test Preparation Inc. makes every reasonable effort to obtain from reliable sources accurate, complete, and timely information about the tests covered in this book. Nevertheless, changes can be made in the tests or the administration of the tests at any time and Complete Test Preparation Inc. makes no representation or warranty, either expressed or implied as to the accuracy, timeliness, or completeness of the information contained in this book. Complete Test Preparation Inc. makes no representations or warranties of any kind, express or implied, about the completeness, accuracy, reliability, suitability or availability with respect to the information contained in this document for any purpose. Any reliance you place on such information is therefore strictly at your own risk.

The author(s) shall not be liable for any loss incurred as a consequence of the use and application, directly or indirectly, of any information presented in this work. Sold with the understanding, the author(s) is not engaged in rendering professional services or advice. If advice or expert assistance is required, the services of a competent professional should be sought.

The company, product and service names used in this publication are for identification purposes only. All trademarks and registered trademarks are the property of their respective owners. Complete Test Preparation Inc. is not affiliated with any educational institution.

**We strongly recommend that students check with exam providers for up-to-date information regarding test content.**

TABE® and the Test of Adult Basic Education is a registered trademark of the MCGRAW-HILL, INC. who are not involved in the production of, and do not endorse this product.

ISBN: 9781772450842

Version 7.6 March 2019

Published by
Complete Test Preparation Inc.
Victoria BC Canada

Visit us on the web at https://www.test-preparation.ca
Printed in the USA

## About Complete Test Preparation Inc.

The Complete Test Preparation Team has been publishing high quality study materials since 2005. Over one million students visit our websites every year, and thousands of students, teachers and parents all over the world (over 100 countries) have purchased our teaching materials, curriculum, study guides and practice tests.

Complete Test Preparation Inc. is committed to providing students with the best study materials and practice tests available on the market. Members of our team combine years of teaching experience, with experienced writers and editors, all with advanced degrees.

## Feedback

We welcome your feedback. Email us at feedback@test-preparation.ca with your comments and suggestions. We carefully review all suggestions and often incorporate reader suggestions into upcoming versions. As a Print on Demand Publisher, we update our products frequently.

https://www.facebook.com/CompleteTestPreparation/

https://www.youtube.com/user/MrTestPreparation

https://www.instagram.com/completetestpreparation/

https://www.pinterest.ca/brians6634/boards/

# Contents

**6**    **Getting Started**
         The TABE® Study Plan    7
         Making a Study Schedule    8

**14**    **Practice Test Questions Set 1**
         Answer Key    62

**78**    **Practice Test Questions Set 2**
         Answer Key    124

**141**    **Conclusion**

# Getting Started

CONGRATULATIONS! By deciding to take the Test of Adult Basic Education (TABE®), you have taken the first step toward a great future! Of course, there is no point in taking this important examination unless you intend to do your best to earn the highest grade you possibly can. That means getting yourself organized and discovering the best approaches, methods and strategies to master the material. Yes, that will require real effort and dedication on your part, but if you are willing to focus your energy and devote the study time necessary, before you know it you will be on you way to a brighter future.

We know that taking on a new endeavour can be scary, and it is easy to feel unsure of where to begin. That's where we come in. This study guide is designed to help you improve your test-taking skills, show you a few tricks of the trade and increase both your competency and confidence.

## The Test of Adult Basic Education®

The TABE® exam is a computer based exam, composed of four sections, reading, computational mathematics, applied mathematics, and language.

| Section | Time | Questions |
|---|---|---|
| Reading | 25 | 25 |
| Computational Math | 15 | 25 |
| Applied Math | 25 | 25 |
| Language | 25 | 25 |

For complete details on the skills evaluated in each section, see the corresponding chapter below.

# GETTING STARTED         7

While we seek to make our guide as comprehensive as possible, note that like all entrance exams, the TABE® Exam might be adjusted at some future point. New material might be added, or content that is no longer relevant or applicable might be removed. It is always a good idea to give the materials you receive when you register to take the TABE® a careful review.

## The TABE® Study Plan

Now that you have made the decision to take the TABE®, it is time to get started. Before you do another thing, you will need to figure out a plan of attack. The very best study tip is to start early! The longer the time period you devote to regular study practice, the more likely you will retain the material and be able to access it quickly. If you thought that 1x20 is the same as 2x10, guess what? It really is not, when it comes to study time. Reviewing material for just an hour per day over the course of 20 days is far better than studying for two hours a day for only 10 days. The more often you revisit a particular piece of information, the better you will know it. Not only will your grasp and understanding be better, but your ability to reach into your brain and quickly and efficiently pull out the tidbit you need, will be greatly enhanced as well.

The great Chinese scholar and philosopher Confucius believed that true knowledge could be defined as knowing what you know and what you do not know. The first step in preparing for the TABE® Exam is to assess your strengths and weaknesses. You may already have an idea of what you know and what you do not know, but evaluating yourself using our Self- Assessment modules for each of the three areas, math, reading comprehension and essay writing, will clarify the details.

**Making a Study Schedule**

To make your study time the most productive, you will need to develop a study plan. The purpose of the plan is to organize all the bits of pieces of information in such a way that you will not feel overwhelmed. Rome was not built in a day, and learning everything you will need to know to pass the TABE® Exam is going to take time, too. Arranging the material you need to learn into manageable chunks is the best way to go. Each study session should make you feel as though you have accomplished your goal, or at least are a little closer, and your goal is simply to learn what you planned to learn during that particular session. Try to organize the content in such a way that each study session builds upon previous ones. That way, you will retain the information, be better able to access it, and review the previous bits and pieces at the same time.

## Self-assessment

**The Best Study Tip!** The very best study tip is to start early! The longer you study regularly, the more you will retain and 'learn' the material. Studying for 1 hour per day for 20 days is far better than studying for 2 hours for 10 days.

**What don't you know?**

The first step is to assess your strengths and weaknesses. You may already have an idea of where your weaknesses are, or you can take our Self-assessment modules for each of the areas, math, reading comprehension and essay writing.

# GETTING STARTED

| Exam Component | Rate from 1 to 5 |
|---|---|
| | |
| **Reading** | |
| Main idea and supporting details | |
| Drawing inferences | |
| | |
| **Mathematics** | |
| Algebra | |
| Estimation | |
| Percent, Decimal, Fractions | |
| Word Problems | |
| Basic Geometry | |
| Word Problems | |

## Making a Study Schedule

**The key to a successful study plan is to divide the material you need to learn into manageable size and learn it, while at the same time reviewing the material that you already know.**

Using the table above, any scores of three or below, mean you need to spend time learning, going over, and practicing this subject area. A score of four means you need to review the material, but you don't have to spend time re-learning. A score of five and you are OK with just an occasional review before the exam.

A score of zero or one means you really do need to work on this and you should allocate the most time and give it the highest priority. Some students prefer a 5-day plan and others a 10-day plan. It also depends on how much time you have until the exam.

Here is an example of a 5-day plan based on an example from the table above:

**Reading:** 1   Study 1 hour everyday – review on last day
**Fractions:** 3   Study 1 hour for 2 days then ½ hour and then review
**Algebra:** 4   Review every second day
**Word Problems (Applied Math) :** 2 Study 1 hour on the first day – then ½ hour everyday
**Basic Geometry:** 5 Review for ½ hour every other day

Using this example, Basic Geometry is good and only needs occasional review. Algebra is good and needs 'some' review. Fractions need a bit of work, grammar and usage needs a lot of work and Reading is very weak and need the most time. Based on this, here is a sample study plan:

## GETTING STARTED

| Day | Subject | Time |
|---|---|---|
| **Monday** | | |
| Study | Reading | 1 hour |
| Study | Word Problems | 1 hour |
| | **½ hour break** | |
| Study | Fractions | 1 hour |
| Review | Algebra | ½ hour |
| **Tuesday** | | |
| Study | Reading | 1 hour |
| Study | Word Problems | ½ hour |
| | **½ hour break** | |
| Study | Fractions | ½ hour |
| Review | Algebra | ½ hour |
| Review | Basic Geometry | ½ hour |
| **Wednesday** | | |
| Study | Reading | 1 hour |
| Study | Word Problems | ½ hour |
| | **½ hour break** | |
| Study | Fractions | ½ hour |
| Review | Basic Geometry | ½ hour |
| **Thursday** | | |
| Study | Reading | ½ hour |
| Study | Word Problems | ½ hour |
| Review | Fractions | ½ hour |
| | **½ hour break** | |
| Review | Basic Geometry | ½ hour |
| Review | Algebra | ½ hour |
| **Friday** | | |
| Review | Reading | ½ hour |
| Review | Word Problems | ½ hour |
| Review | Fractions | ½ hour |
| | **½ hour break** | |
| Review | Algebra | ½ hour |
| Review | Word Problems | ½ hour |

Using this example, adapt the study plan to your own schedule. This schedule assumes 2 ½ - 3 hours available to study everyday for a 5 day period.

First, write out what you need to study and how much. Next figure out how many days you have before the test. Note, do NOT study on the last day before the test. On the last day before the test, you won't learn anything and will probably only confuse yourself.

Make a table with the days before the test and the number of hours you have available to study each day. We suggest working with 1 hour and ½ hour time slots.

Start filling in the blanks, with the subjects you need to study the most getting the most time and the most regular time slots (i.e. everyday) and the subjects that you know getting the least time (e.g. ½ hour every other day, or every 3rd day).

## Tips for making a schedule

**Once you make a schedule, stick with it!** Make your study sessions reasonable. If you make a study schedule and don't stick with it, you set yourself up for failure. Instead, schedule study sessions that are a bit shorter and set yourself up for success! Make sure your study sessions are do-able. Studying is hard work but after you pass, you can party and take a break!

**Schedule breaks.** Breaks are just as important as study time. Work out a rotation of studying and breaks that works for you.

**Build up study time.** If you find it hard to sit still and study for 1 hour straight through, build up to it. Start with 20 minutes, and then take a break. Once you get used to 20-minute study sessions, increase the time to 30 minutes. Gradually work you way up to 1 hour.

**40 minutes to 1 hour is optimal**. Studying for longer than this is tiring and not productive. Studying for shorter isn't long enough to be productive.

# Getting Started     13

**Studying Math.** Studying Math is different from studying other subjects because you use a different part of your brain. The best way to study math is to practice everyday. This will train your mind to think in a mathematical way. If you miss a day or days, the mathematical mind-set is gone and you have to start all over again to build it up.

Study and practice math everyday for at least 5 days before the exam.

# Practice Test Questions Set 1

The questions below are not exactly the same as you will find on the TABE® - that would be too easy! And nobody knows what the questions will be and they change all the time. Below are general questions that cover the same subject areas as the TABE®. So while the format and exact wording of the questions may differ slightly, and change from year to year, if you can answer the questions below, you will have no problem with the TABE®.

For the best results, take these Practice Test Questions as if it were the real exam. Set aside time when you will not be disturbed, and a location that is quiet and free of distractions. Read the instructions carefully, read each question carefully, and answer to the best of your ability.
Use the bubble answer sheets provided. When you have completed the Practice Questions, check your answer against the Answer Key and read the explanation provided.

Do not attempt more than one set of practice test questions in one day. After completing the first practice test, wait two or three days before attempting the second set of questions.

# Practice Test Questions 1

**Reading**

|    | A | B | C | D | E |    | A | B | C | D | E |
|----|---|---|---|---|---|----|---|---|---|---|---|
| 1  | ○ | ○ | ○ | ○ | ○ | 21 | ○ | ○ | ○ | ○ | ○ |
| 2  | ○ | ○ | ○ | ○ | ○ | 22 | ○ | ○ | ○ | ○ | ○ |
| 3  | ○ | ○ | ○ | ○ | ○ | 23 | ○ | ○ | ○ | ○ | ○ |
| 4  | ○ | ○ | ○ | ○ | ○ | 24 | ○ | ○ | ○ | ○ | ○ |
| 5  | ○ | ○ | ○ | ○ | ○ | 25 | ○ | ○ | ○ | ○ | ○ |
| 6  | ○ | ○ | ○ | ○ | ○ |    |   |   |   |   |   |
| 7  | ○ | ○ | ○ | ○ | ○ |    |   |   |   |   |   |
| 8  | ○ | ○ | ○ | ○ | ○ |    |   |   |   |   |   |
| 9  | ○ | ○ | ○ | ○ | ○ |    |   |   |   |   |   |
| 10 | ○ | ○ | ○ | ○ | ○ |    |   |   |   |   |   |
| 11 | ○ | ○ | ○ | ○ | ○ |    |   |   |   |   |   |
| 12 | ○ | ○ | ○ | ○ | ○ |    |   |   |   |   |   |
| 13 | ○ | ○ | ○ | ○ | ○ |    |   |   |   |   |   |
| 14 | ○ | ○ | ○ | ○ | ○ |    |   |   |   |   |   |
| 15 | ○ | ○ | ○ | ○ | ○ |    |   |   |   |   |   |
| 16 | ○ | ○ | ○ | ○ | ○ |    |   |   |   |   |   |
| 17 | ○ | ○ | ○ | ○ | ○ |    |   |   |   |   |   |
| 18 | ○ | ○ | ○ | ○ | ○ |    |   |   |   |   |   |
| 19 | ○ | ○ | ○ | ○ | ○ |    |   |   |   |   |   |
| 20 | ○ | ○ | ○ | ○ | ○ |    |   |   |   |   |   |

# TABE® Skill Practice

## Computational Mathematics

|     | A | B | C | D | E |     | A | B | C | D | E |
|-----|---|---|---|---|---|-----|---|---|---|---|---|
| 1   | ○ | ○ | ○ | ○ | ○ | 21  | ○ | ○ | ○ | ○ | ○ |
| 2   | ○ | ○ | ○ | ○ | ○ | 22  | ○ | ○ | ○ | ○ | ○ |
| 3   | ○ | ○ | ○ | ○ | ○ | 23  | ○ | ○ | ○ | ○ | ○ |
| 4   | ○ | ○ | ○ | ○ | ○ | 24  | ○ | ○ | ○ | ○ | ○ |
| 5   | ○ | ○ | ○ | ○ | ○ | 25  | ○ | ○ | ○ | ○ | ○ |
| 6   | ○ | ○ | ○ | ○ | ○ |     |   |   |   |   |   |
| 7   | ○ | ○ | ○ | ○ | ○ |     |   |   |   |   |   |
| 8   | ○ | ○ | ○ | ○ | ○ |     |   |   |   |   |   |
| 9   | ○ | ○ | ○ | ○ | ○ |     |   |   |   |   |   |
| 10  | ○ | ○ | ○ | ○ | ○ |     |   |   |   |   |   |
| 11  | ○ | ○ | ○ | ○ | ○ |     |   |   |   |   |   |
| 12  | ○ | ○ | ○ | ○ | ○ |     |   |   |   |   |   |
| 13  | ○ | ○ | ○ | ○ | ○ |     |   |   |   |   |   |
| 14  | ○ | ○ | ○ | ○ | ○ |     |   |   |   |   |   |
| 15  | ○ | ○ | ○ | ○ | ○ |     |   |   |   |   |   |
| 16  | ○ | ○ | ○ | ○ | ○ |     |   |   |   |   |   |
| 17  | ○ | ○ | ○ | ○ | ○ |     |   |   |   |   |   |
| 18  | ○ | ○ | ○ | ○ | ○ |     |   |   |   |   |   |
| 19  | ○ | ○ | ○ | ○ | ○ |     |   |   |   |   |   |
| 20  | ○ | ○ | ○ | ○ | ○ |     |   |   |   |   |   |

# Practice Test Questions 1

## Applied Mathematics

|    | A | B | C | D | E |     |    | A | B | C | D | E |
|----|---|---|---|---|---|-----|----|---|---|---|---|---|
| 1  | ○ | ○ | ○ | ○ | ○ |     | 21 | ○ | ○ | ○ | ○ | ○ |
| 2  | ○ | ○ | ○ | ○ | ○ |     | 22 | ○ | ○ | ○ | ○ | ○ |
| 3  | ○ | ○ | ○ | ○ | ○ |     | 23 | ○ | ○ | ○ | ○ | ○ |
| 4  | ○ | ○ | ○ | ○ | ○ |     | 24 | ○ | ○ | ○ | ○ | ○ |
| 5  | ○ | ○ | ○ | ○ | ○ |     | 25 | ○ | ○ | ○ | ○ | ○ |
| 6  | ○ | ○ | ○ | ○ | ○ |     |    |   |   |   |   |   |
| 7  | ○ | ○ | ○ | ○ | ○ |     |    |   |   |   |   |   |
| 8  | ○ | ○ | ○ | ○ | ○ |     |    |   |   |   |   |   |
| 9  | ○ | ○ | ○ | ○ | ○ |     |    |   |   |   |   |   |
| 10 | ○ | ○ | ○ | ○ | ○ |     |    |   |   |   |   |   |
| 11 | ○ | ○ | ○ | ○ | ○ |     |    |   |   |   |   |   |
| 12 | ○ | ○ | ○ | ○ | ○ |     |    |   |   |   |   |   |
| 13 | ○ | ○ | ○ | ○ | ○ |     |    |   |   |   |   |   |
| 14 | ○ | ○ | ○ | ○ | ○ |     |    |   |   |   |   |   |
| 15 | ○ | ○ | ○ | ○ | ○ |     |    |   |   |   |   |   |
| 16 | ○ | ○ | ○ | ○ | ○ |     |    |   |   |   |   |   |
| 17 | ○ | ○ | ○ | ○ | ○ |     |    |   |   |   |   |   |
| 18 | ○ | ○ | ○ | ○ | ○ |     |    |   |   |   |   |   |
| 19 | ○ | ○ | ○ | ○ | ○ |     |    |   |   |   |   |   |
| 20 | ○ | ○ | ○ | ○ | ○ |     |    |   |   |   |   |   |

## Language

|    | A | B | C | D | E |    | A | B | C | D | E |
|----|---|---|---|---|---|----|---|---|---|---|---|
| 1  | ○ | ○ | ○ | ○ | ○ | 21 | ○ | ○ | ○ | ○ | ○ |
| 2  | ○ | ○ | ○ | ○ | ○ | 22 | ○ | ○ | ○ | ○ | ○ |
| 3  | ○ | ○ | ○ | ○ | ○ | 23 | ○ | ○ | ○ | ○ | ○ |
| 4  | ○ | ○ | ○ | ○ | ○ | 24 | ○ | ○ | ○ | ○ | ○ |
| 5  | ○ | ○ | ○ | ○ | ○ | 25 | ○ | ○ | ○ | ○ | ○ |
| 6  | ○ | ○ | ○ | ○ | ○ | 26 | ○ | ○ | ○ | ○ | ○ |
| 7  | ○ | ○ | ○ | ○ | ○ | 27 | ○ | ○ | ○ | ○ | ○ |
| 8  | ○ | ○ | ○ | ○ | ○ | 28 | ○ | ○ | ○ | ○ | ○ |
| 9  | ○ | ○ | ○ | ○ | ○ | 29 | ○ | ○ | ○ | ○ | ○ |
| 10 | ○ | ○ | ○ | ○ | ○ | 30 | ○ | ○ | ○ | ○ | ○ |
| 11 | ○ | ○ | ○ | ○ | ○ | 31 | ○ | ○ | ○ | ○ | ○ |
| 12 | ○ | ○ | ○ | ○ | ○ | 32 | ○ | ○ | ○ | ○ | ○ |
| 13 | ○ | ○ | ○ | ○ | ○ | 33 | ○ | ○ | ○ | ○ | ○ |
| 14 | ○ | ○ | ○ | ○ | ○ | 34 | ○ | ○ | ○ | ○ | ○ |
| 15 | ○ | ○ | ○ | ○ | ○ | 35 | ○ | ○ | ○ | ○ | ○ |
| 16 | ○ | ○ | ○ | ○ | ○ | 36 | ○ | ○ | ○ | ○ | ○ |
| 17 | ○ | ○ | ○ | ○ | ○ | 37 | ○ | ○ | ○ | ○ | ○ |
| 18 | ○ | ○ | ○ | ○ | ○ | 38 | ○ | ○ | ○ | ○ | ○ |
| 19 | ○ | ○ | ○ | ○ | ○ | 39 | ○ | ○ | ○ | ○ | ○ |
| 20 | ○ | ○ | ○ | ○ | ○ | 40 | ○ | ○ | ○ | ○ | ○ |

# Practice Test Questions 1

## Reading and Language Arts

**Directions:** The following questions are based on several reading passages. A series of questions follow each passage. Read each passage carefully, and then answer the questions based on it. You may reread the passage as often as you wish. When you have finished answering the questions based on one passage, go right onto the next passage. Choose the best answer based on the information given and implied.

**Questions 1 – 4 refer to the following passage.**

**Passage 1 - The Life of Helen Keller**

Many people have heard of Helen Keller. She is famous because she was unable to see or hear, but learned to speak and read and went onto attend college and earn a degree. Her life is a very interesting story, one that she developed into an autobiography, which was then adapted into both a stage play and a movie. How did Helen Keller overcome her disabilities to become a famous woman? Read onto find out. Helen Keller was not born blind and deaf. When she was a small baby, she had a very high fever for several days. As a result of her sudden illness, baby Helen lost her eyesight and her hearing. Because she was so young when she went deaf and blind, Helen Keller never had any recollection of being able to see or hear. Since she could not hear, she could not learn to talk. Since she could not see, it was difficult for her to move around. For the first six years of her life, her world was very still and dark.

Imagine what Helen's childhood was like. She could not hear her mother's voice. She could not see the beauty of her parent's farm. She could not recognize who was giving her a hug, or a bath or even where her bedroom was each night. More sad, she could not communicate with her parents in any way. She could not express her feelings or tell them the things she wanted. It must have been a very sad childhood.

When Helen was six years old, her parents hired her a teacher named Anne Sullivan. Anne was a young woman who was almost blind. However, she could hear and she could read Braille, so she was a perfect teacher for young Helen. At first, Anne had a very hard time teaching Helen anything. She described her first impression of Helen as a "wild thing, not a child." Helen did not like Anne at first either. She bit and hit Anne when Anne tried to teach her. However, the two of them eventually came to have a great deal of love and respect.

Anne taught Helen to hear by putting her hands on people's throats. She could feel the sounds that people made. In time, Helen learned to feel what people said. Next, Anne taught Helen to read Braille, which is a way that books are written for the blind. Finally, Anne taught Helen to talk. Although Helen did learn to talk, it was hard for anyone but Anne to understand her.

As Helen grew older, more and more people were amazed by her story. She went to college and wrote books about her life. She gave talks to the public, with Anne at her side, translating her words. Today, both Anne Sullivan and Helen Keller are famous women who are respected for their lives' work.

**1. Helen Keller could not see and hear and so, what was her biggest problem in childhood?**

    a. Inability to communicate

    b. Inability to walk

    c. Inability to play

    d. Inability to eat

**2. Helen learned to hear by feeling the vibrations people made when they spoke. What were these vibrations were felt through?**

    a. Mouth

    b. Throat

    c. Ears

    d. Lips

## Practice Test Questions 1

**3. From the passage, we can infer that Anne Sullivan was a patient teacher. We can infer this because**

    a. Helen hit and bit her and Anne still remained her teacher.

    b. Anne taught Helen to read only.

    c. Anne was hard of hearing too.

    d. Anne wanted to be a teacher.

**4. Helen Keller learned to speak but Anne translated her words when she spoke in public. The reason Helen needed a translator was because**

    a. Helen spoke another language.

    b. Helen's words were hard for people to understand.

    c. Helen spoke very quietly.

    d. Helen did not speak but only used sign language.

**Questions 5 – 7 refer to the following passage.**

**Passage 2 - Ways Characters Communicate in Theater**

Playwrights give their characters voices in a way that gives depth and added meaning to what happens on stage during their play. There are different types of speech in scripts that allow characters to talk with themselves, with other characters, and even with the audience.

It is very unique to theater that characters may talk "to themselves." When characters do this, the speech they give is called a soliloquy. Soliloquies are usually poetic, introspective, moving, and can tell audience members about the feelings, motivations, or suspicions of an individual character without that character having to reveal them to other characters on stage. "To be or not to be" is a famous soliloquy given by Hamlet as he considers difficult but important themes, such as life and death.

The most common type of communication in plays is when one character is speaking to another or a group of other characters. This is generally called dialogue, but can also be called monologue if one character speaks without being interrupted for a long time. It is not necessarily the most important type of communication, but it is the most common because the plot of the play cannot really progress without it.

Lastly, and most unique to theater (although it has been used somewhat in film) is when a character speaks directly to the audience. This is called an aside, and scripts usually specifically direct actors to do this. Asides are usually comical, an inside joke between the character and the audience, and very short. The actor will usually face the audience when delivering them, even if it's for a moment, so the audience can recognize this move as an aside.

All three of these types of communication are important to the art of theater, and have been perfected by famous playwrights like Shakespeare. Understanding these types of communication can help an audience member grasp what is artful about the script and action of a play.

**5. According to the passage, characters in plays communicate to**

    a. move the plot forward

    b. show the private thoughts and feelings of one character

    c. make the audience laugh

    d. add beauty and artistry to the play

**6. When Hamlet delivers "To be or not to be," he can most likely be described as**

    a. solitary

    b. thoughtful

    c. dramatic

    d. hopeless

# Practice Test Questions 1    23

**7. The author uses parentheses to punctuate "although it has been used somewhat in film,"**

    a. to show that films are less important

    b. instead of using commas so that the sentence is not interrupted

    c. because parenthesis help separate details that are not as important

    d. to show that films are not as artistic

**Questions 8 – 10 refer to the following passage.**

**Passage 3 - Low Blood Sugar**

As the name suggest, low blood sugar is low sugar levels in the bloodstream. This can occur when you have not eaten properly and undertake strenuous activity, or, when you are very hungry. When Low blood sugar occurs regularly and is ongoing, it is a medical condition called hypoglycemia. This condition can occur in diabetics and in healthy adults.

Causes of low blood sugar can include excessive alcohol consumption, metabolic problems, stomach surgery, pancreas, liver or kidneys problems, as well as a side-effect of some medications.

**Symptoms**

There are different symptoms depending on the severity of the case.

Mild hypoglycemia can lead to feelings of nausea and hunger. The patient may also feel nervous, jittery and have fast heart beats. Sweaty skin, clammy and cold skin are likely symptoms.
Moderate hypoglycemia can result in a short temper, confusion, nervousness, fear and blurring of vision. The patient may feel weak and unsteady.

Severe cases of hypoglycemia can lead to seizures, coma,

fainting spells, nightmares, headaches, excessive sweats and severe tiredness.

**Diagnosis of low blood sugar**

A doctor can diagnosis this medical condition by asking the patient questions and testing blood and urine samples. Home testing kits are available for patients to monitor blood sugar levels. It is important to see a qualified doctor though. The doctor can administer tests to ensure that will safely rule out other medical conditions that could affect blood sugar levels.

**Treatment**

Quick treatments include drinking or eating foods and drinks with high sugar contents. Good examples include soda, fruit juice, hard candy and raisins. Glucose energy tablets can also help. Doctors may also recommend medications and well as changes in diet and exercise routine to treat chronic low blood sugar.

**8. Based on the article, which of the following is true?**

    a. Low blood sugar can happen to anyone.

    b. Low blood sugar only happens to diabetics.

    c. Low blood sugar can occur even.

    d. None of the statements are true.

**9. Which of the following are the author's opinion?**

    a. Quick treatments include drinking or eating foods and drinks with high sugar contents.

    b. None of the statements are opinions.

    c. This condition can occur in diabetics and also in healthy adults.

    d. There are different symptoms depending on the severity of the case

**10. What is the author's purpose?**

    a. To inform

    b. To persuade

    c. To entertain

    d. To analyze

**11. Which of the following is not a detail?**

    a. A doctor can diagnosis this medical condition by asking the patient questions and testing.

    b. A doctor will test blood and urine samples.

    c. Glucose energy tablets can also help.

    d. Home test kits monitor blood sugar levels.

    d. None of the above.

**Questions 12 – 15 refer to the following passage.**

**How To Get A Good Nights Sleep**

Sleep is just as essential for healthy living as water, air and food. Sleep allows the body to rest and replenish depleted energy levels. Sometimes we may, for various reasons, experience difficulty sleeping which has a serious effect on our health. Those who have prolonged sleeping problems are facing a serious medical condition and should see a qualified doctor when possible for help. Here is simple guide that can help you sleep better at night.

Try to create a natural pattern of waking up and sleeping around the same time everyday. This means avoiding going to bed too early and oversleeping past your usual wake up time. Going to bed and getting up at radically different times everyday confuses your body clock. Try to establish a natural rhythm as much as you can.

Exercises and a bit of physical activity can help you sleep

better at night. If you are having problem sleeping, try to be as active as you can during the day. If you are tired from physical activity, falling asleep is a natural and easy process for your body. If you remain inactive during the day, you will find it harder to sleep properly at night. Try walking, jogging, swimming or simple stretches as you get close to your bed time.

Afternoon naps are great to refresh you during the day, but they may also keep you awake at night. If you feel sleepy during the day, get up, take a walk and get busy to keep from sleeping. Stretching is a good way to increase blood flow to the brain and keep you alert so that you don't sleep during the day. This will help you sleep better night.

> A warm bath or a glass of milk in the evening can help your body relax and prepare for sleep. A cold bath will wake you up and keep you up for several hours. Also avoid eating too late before bed.

**12. How would you describe this sentence?**

    a. A recommendation

    b. An opinion

    c. A fact

    d. A diagnosis

**13. Which of the following is an alternative title for this article?**

    a. Exercise and a good night's sleep

    b. Benefits of a good night's sleep

    c. Tips for a good night's sleep

    d. Lack of sleep is a serious medical condition

# Practice Test Questions 1

**14. Which of the following cannot be inferred from this article?**

   a. Biking is helpful for getting a good night's sleep

   b. Mental activity is helpful for getting a good night's sleep

   c. Eating bedtime snacks is not recommended

   d. Getting up at the same time is helpful for a good night's sleep

**15. What is a disadvantage of taking naps?**

   a. They may keep you awake.

   b. There are no disadvantages

   c. They may help you sleep better

   d. They may affect your diet

**Question 16 refers to the following Table of Contents.**

**Contents**

    Science Self-assessment 81
    Answer Key 91
    Science Tutorials 96
    Scientific Method 96
    Biology 99
    Heredity: Genes and Mutation 104
    Classification 108
    Ecology 110
    Chemistry 112
    Energy: Kinetic and Mechanical 126
    Energy: Work and Power 130
    Force: Newton's Three Laws 132

16. Consider the table of contents above. What page would you find information about natural selection and adaptation?

    a. 81
    b. 90
    c. 110
    d. 132

**Questions 17 – 19 refer to the following passage.**

**Passage 5 - Pearl Harbor**

A Day That Will Live in Infamy! Attack on Pearl Harbor
In 1941, the world was at war. The United States was trying very hard to keep itself out of the conflict. In Europe, the countries of Germany and Italy had formed an alliance to expand their land and territory. Germany had already taken over Poland, Denmark, and parts of France. They were heading next toward England and due to all the fighting in Europe, there were battles taking place as far south as North Africa, where the German and Italian armies were fighting the British.

This got even worse when the Asian nation of Japan formed an alliance with Germany and Italy. Together, the three countries called themselves, the AXIS. Now, the war was in the Pacific as well as in Europe and Northern Africa. A great deal of Americans felt that perhaps now was the time for the United States to join with its ally, Great Britain and stop the Axis from taking over more regions of the world.

In 1941, Franklin Roosevelt was President of the United States. His fear at the time was that Japan would try to take over many countries in Asia. He did not want to see that happen, so he moved some of the United States warships that had been stationed in San Diego, to the military base at Pearl Harbor, in Honolulu, Hawaii.

Japan quietly plotted their attack. They waited until the

# PRACTICE TEST QUESTIONS 1    29

early hours of the morning on Sunday, December 7, 1941. Then, 350 Japanese war plans began to drop bombs on the U.S. ships at Pearl Harbor. The first bombs fell at 7:48 am and a mere 90 minutes later, the attack was over. Pearl Harbor was decimated. 8 battleships were damaged. Eleven ships were sunk and 300 U.S. planes were destroyed. Most devastating was the loss of life 2,400 U.S. military members was killed in the attack and 1, 282 were injured.

President Roosevelt addressed the country via the radio and said "Today is a day that will live in infamy." He asked Congress to declare war on Japan. War was declared on Japan on December 8th and on Germany and Italy on December 11th. The United States had entered World War Two.

**17. After reading the passage, what can we infer infamy means?**

   a. Famous

   b. Remembered in a good way

   c. Remembered in a bad way

   d. Easily forgotten

**18. What three countries formed the Axis?**

   a. Italy, England, Germany

   b. United States, England, Italy

   c. Germany, Japan, Italy

   d. Germany, Japan, United States

**19. What do you think was President Roosevelt's reason for moving warships to Pearl Harbor?**

   a. He feared Japan would bomb San Diego

   b. He knew Japan was going to attack Pearl Harbor

   c. He was planning to attack Japan

   d. He wanted to try and protect Asian countries from Japanese takeover

**20. Why do you think Japan chose a Sunday morning at 7:48 am for their attack?**

    a. They knew the military slept late

    b. There is a law against bombing countries on a Sunday

    c. They wanted the attack to catch people by surprise

    d. That was the only free time they had to attack.

**Questions 21 - 24 refer to the following recipe.**

**If You Have Allergies, You're Not Alone**

People who experience allergies might joke that their immune systems have let them down or are seriously lacking. Truthfully though, people who experience allergic reactions or allergy symptoms during certain times of the year have heightened immune systems that are, "better" than those of people who have perfectly healthy but less militant immune systems.

Still, when a person has an allergic reaction, they are having an adverse reaction to a substance that is considered normal to most people. Mild allergic reactions usually have symptoms like itching, runny nose, red eyes, or bumps or discoloration of the skin. More serious allergic reactions, such as those to animal and insect poisons or certain foods, may result in the closing of the throat, swelling of the eyes, low blood pressure, inability to breath, and can even be fatal.

Different treatments help different allergies, and which one a person uses depends on the nature and severity of the allergy. It is recommended to patients with severe allergies to take extra precautions, such as carrying an EpiPen, which treats anaphylactic shock and may prevent death, always in order for the remedy to be readily available and more effective. When an allergy is not so severe, treatments may be used just relieve a person of uncomfortable symptoms. Over the counter allergy medicines treat milder symptoms, and can be bought at any grocery store and used in moderation to help people with allergies live normally.

# Practice Test Questions 1

There are many tests available to assess whether a person has allergies or what they may be allergic to, and advances in these tests and the medicine used to treat patients continues to improve. Despite this fact, allergies still affect many people throughout the year or even every day. Medicines used to treat allergies have side effects of their own, and it is difficult to bring the body into balance with the use of medicine. Regardless, many of those who live with allergies are grateful for what is available and find it useful in maintaining their lifestyles.

**21. According to this passage, it can be understood that the word "militant" belongs in a group with the words:**

    a. sickly, ailing, faint

    b. strength, power, vigor

    c. active, fighting, warring

    d. worn, tired, breaking down

**22. The author says that "medicines used to treat allergies have side-effects of their own" to**

    a. point out that doctors aren't very good at diagnosing and treating allergies

    b. argue that because of the large number of people with allergies, a cure will never be found

    c. explain that allergy medicines aren't cures and some compromise must be made

    d. argue that more wholesome remedies should be researched and medicines banned

**23. It can be inferred that _____ recommend that some people with allergies carry medicine with them.**

    a. the author

    b. doctors

    c. the makers of EpiPen

    d. people with allergies

**24. The author has written this passage to**

    a. inform readers on symptoms of allergies so people with allergies can get help

    b. persuade readers to be proud of having allergies

    c. inform readers on different remedies so people with allergies receive the right help

    d. describe different types of allergies, their symptoms, and their remedies

**Questions 25 – 26 refer to the following email.**

SUBJECT: MEDICAL STAFF CHANGES

To all staff:

This email is to advise you of a paper on recommended medical staff changes has been posted to the Human Resources website.

The contents are of primary interest to medical staff, other staff may be interested in reading it, particularly those in medical support roles.

The paper deals with several major issues:

    1. Improving our ability to attract top quality staff to the hospital, and retain our existing staff. These changes will make our position and departmental names internationally recognizable and comparable with North American and North Asian departments and positions.

    2. Improving our ability to attract top quality staff by introducing greater flexibility in the departmental structure.

    3. General comments on issues to be further discussed in relation to research staff.

## Practice Test Questions 1    33

The changes outlined in this paper are significant. I encourage you to read the document and send to me any comments you may have, so that it can be enhanced and improved.

Gordon Simms
Administrator,
Seven Oaks Regional Hospital

**25. Are all hospital staff required to read the document posted to the
Human Resources website?**

    a. Yes all staff are required to read the document.

    b. No, reading the document is optional.

    c. Only medical staff are required to read the document.

    d. none of the above are correct.

# Computational Mathematics

**1. What fraction of $1500 is $75?**

    a. 1/14
    b. 3/5
    c. 7/10
    d. 1/20

**2. Estimate 215 x 65.**

    a. 1,350
    b. 13,500
    c. 103,500
    d. 3,500

**3. Below is the attendance for a class of 45.**

| Day | Number of Absent Students |
|---|---|
| Monday | 5 |
| Tuesday | 9 |
| Wednesday | 4 |
| Thursday | 10 |
| Friday | 6 |

**What is the average attendance for the week?**

    a. 88%
    b. 85%
    c. 81%
    d. 77%

**4. 2/3 – 2/5 =**

    a. 4/10
    b. 1/15
    c. 3/7
    d. 4/15

**5. Express 0.27 + 0.33 as a fraction.**

    a. 3/6
    b. 4/7
    c. 3/5
    d. 2/7

# PRACTICE TEST QUESTIONS 1     35

6. $7^5 - 3^5 =$

    a. 15,000
    b. 16,564
    c. 15,800
    d. 15,007

7. What is 2/4 X 3/4 reduced to lowest terms?

    a. 6/12
    b. 3/8
    c. 6/16
    d. 3/4

8. Solve the following equation 4(y + 6) = 3y + 30

    a. y = 20
    b. y = 6
    c. y = 30/7
    d. y = 30

9. 2/3 of 60 + 1/5 of 75 =

    a. 45
    b. 55
    c. 15
    d. 50

10. What is 1/3 of 3/4?

    a. 1/4
    b. 1/3
    c. 2/3
    d. 3/4

11. What is (3.13 + 7.87) X 5?

   a. 65
   b. 50
   c. 45
   d. 55

12. Express 5 x 5 x 5 x 5 x 5 x 5 in exponential form.

   a. $5^6$
   b. $10^6$
   c. $5^{16}$
   d. $5^3$

13. Express 9 x 9 x 9 in exponential form and standard form.

   a. $9^3 = 719$
   b. $9^3 = 629$
   c. $9^3 = 729$
   d. $10^3 = 729$

14. If y = 4 and x = 3, solve $yx^3$

   a. -108
   b. 108
   c. 27
   d. 4

15. Divide 0.524 by $10^3$

   a. 0.0524
   b. 0.000524
   c. 0.00524
   d. 524

# Practice Test Questions 1

16. Solve 3x − 27 = 0

    a. x = 24
    b. x = 30
    c. x = 9
    d. x = 21

17. Which of the following is between 7/11 and 5/7?

    a. 0.6
    b. 13/17
    c. 2/3
    d. 11/15

18. Solve: 0.25 + 0.65

    a. 1/2
    b. 9/10
    c. 4/7
    d. 2/9

19. 389 + 454 =

    a. 853
    b. 833
    c. 843
    d. 863

20. 9,177 + 7,204 =

    a. 16,4712
    b. 16,371
    c. 16,381
    d. 15,412

**21.** 2,199 + 5,832 =

    a. 8,331
    b. 8,041
    c. 8,141
    d. 8,031

**22.** 8,390 - 5,239 =

    a. 3,261
    b. 3,151
    c. 3,161
    d. 3,101

**23.** 643 - 587 =

    a. 56
    b. 66
    c. 46
    d. 55

**24.** 3,406 - 2,767 =

    a. 629
    b. 720
    c. 639
    d. 649

**25.** 149 × 7 =

    a. 1032
    b. 1043
    c. 1059
    d. 1063

# Practice Test Questions 1

## Applied Mathematics

1. A square box measures 20 cm long and 20 cm wide and 20 cm high. What is the volume of the box?

    a. 60 cm³
    b. 20,000 cm³
    c. 4,000 cm³
    d. 8,000 cm³

2. A worker's weekly salary was increased by 30%. If his new salary is $150, what was his old salary?

    a. $120.00
    b. $99.15
    c. $109.00
    d. $115.40

3. Mr. Jones runs a factory. His total assets are $256,800 which consists of a building worth $80,500, machinery worth $125.000 and $51,300 cash. After one year what will be the value of his total assets if he has additional cash of $75,600 and the value of his building has increased by 10% per year, and his machinery depreciated by 20%?

    a. $243,450
    b. $252,450
    c. $315,450
    d. $272,350

4. Brad has agreed to buy everyone a Coke. Each drink costs $1.89, and there are 5 friends. Estimate Brad's cost.

   a. $7
   b. $8
   c. $10
   d. $12

5. The manager of a weaving factory estimates that if 10 machines run at 100% efficiency for 8 hours, they will produce 1450 meters of cloth. Due to some technical problems, 4 machines run of 95% efficiency and the remaining 6 at 90% efficiency. How many meters of cloth can these machines will produce in 8 hours?

   a. 1334 meters
   b. 1310 meters
   c. 1300 meters
   d. 1285 meters

6. My current pay is 'x' dollars. Every month it is increased 0.5%. After 'y' months, what will my pay be?

   a. X + 0.005xy
   b. 1.002xy
   c. X + 1.005xy/y
   d. X + 1.005xy

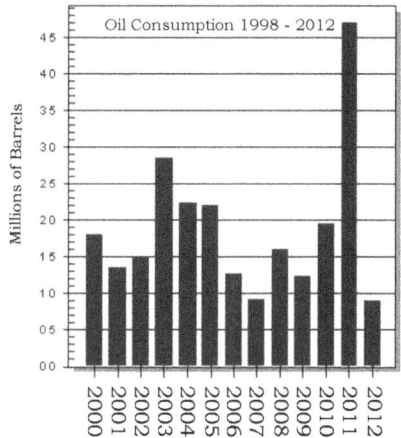

7. The graph above shows oil consumption in millions of barrels for the period, 1998 - 2012. What year did oil consumption peak?

   a. 2011
   b. 2010
   c. 2008
   d. 2009

8. In a local election at polling station A, 945 voters cast their vote out of 1270 registered voters. At polling station B, 860 cast their vote out of 1050 registered voters and at station C, 1210 cast their vote out of 1440 registered voters. What is the total turnout from all three polling stations?

   a. 70%
   b. 74%
   c. 76%
   d. 80%

9. A pet store sold $19,304.56 worth of merchandise in June. If the cost of products sold was $5,284.34, employees were paid $8,384.76, and rent was $2,920.00, how much profit did the store make in June?

    a. $5,635.46
    b. $2,714.46
    c. $14,020.22
    d. $10,019.80
    e) $16,383.57

10. A small lot has a perimeter of 100 feet. What's the area, expressed in square feet?

    a. We cannot tell from this information.
    b. 10 ft$^2$
    c. 400 ft$^2$
    d. 25 ft$^2$

11. John is a barber and receives 40% of the amount paid by each of his customers. John gets all of any tips paid to him. If a customer pays $8.50 for a haircut and pays a tip of $1.30, how much money goes to John?

    a. $3.92
    b. $4.70
    c. $5.30
    d. $6.40

# PRACTICE TEST QUESTIONS 1 — 43

12. Mr. Jones bought 5 children's tickets and 9 adult tickets to the zoo. He paid a total of $67. Mr. Jackson paid $38.50 for 7 adult tickets. What is the cost of each type of ticket?

   a. adult = $13.40 and children = $47.44
   b. adult = $7.44 and children = $13.40
   c. adult = $3.50 and children = $5.50
   d. adult = $5.50 and children = $3.50

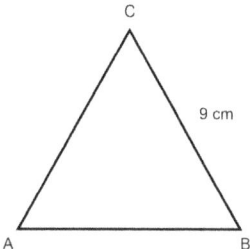

13. What is the perimeter of the equilateral △ABC above?

   a. 18 cm
   b. 12 cm
   c. 27 cm
   d. 15 cm

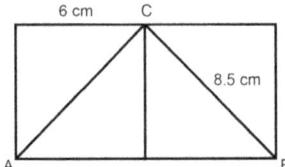

Note: Figure not drawn to scale

**14. Assuming the 2 quadrangles above are identical rectangles, what is the perimeter of △ABC in the above shape?**

    a. 25.5 cm
    b. 27 cm
    c. 30 cm
    d. 29 cm

**15. A woman spent 15% of her income on an item and ends up with $120. What percentage of her income is left?**

    a. 12%
    b. 85%
    c. 75%
    d. 95%

**16. A rectangular box measures 10 cm long and 8 cm wide and 10 cm high. What is the volume of the box?**

    a. 28 cm³
    b. 2000 cm³
    c. 400 cm³
    d. 800 cm³

# PRACTICE TEST QUESTIONS 1          45

**17.** At the beginning of 2009, Marilyn invested $5,000 in a savings account. The account pays 4% interest per year. At the end 2 years, how much did Marilyn have in the account?

    a. $5,200
    b. $5,408
    c. $5,110
    d. $7,000

**18.** A distributor purchased 550 kilograms of potatoes for $165. He distributed these at a rate of $6.4 per 20 kilograms to 15 shops, $3.4 per 10 kilograms to 12 shops and the remainder at $1.8 per 5 kilograms. If his total distribution cost is $10, what will his profit be?

    a. $10.4
    b. $13.6
    c. $14.9
    d. $23.4

**19.** A car covers a distance in 3.5 hours with an average speed of 60 km/hr. How much time in hours will a motorbike take to cover this distance with average speed of 40km/hr?

    a. 6 hours
    b. 5 hours
    c. 5.5 hours
    d. 5.25 hours

**20.** Write 51.738 to the nearest 100th.

    a. 51.735
    b. 51.7
    c. 51.73
    d. 51.74

21. What is the ratio between 2 gold coins, 6 silver coins and 12 bronze coins?

    a. 2:3:4
    b. 1:2:4
    c. 1:3:6
    d. 2:3:4

22. Choose the expression the figure represents.

    a. X < 1
    b. X < 1
    c. X > 1
    d. X ≠ 1

23. Choose the expression the figure represents.

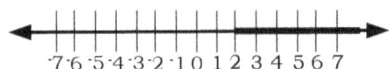

    a. X > 2
    b. X > 2
    c. X < 2
    d. X ≠ 2

# Practice Test Questions 1    47

24. Convert 7,892,000,000 to scientific notation.

    a. $7.892 \times 10^{10}$
    b. $7.892 \times 10^{-9}$
    c. $7.892 \times 10^{9}$
    d. $0.7892 \times 10^{11}$

25. Consider the following sequence:

+ * + * | * + * + | * * + * | + + __ __

    a. + *
    b. * *
    c. + +
    d. * +

# English

**For questions 1 - 5, fill in the blank with the correct punctuation.**

1. Watch out for the broken glass \_\_\_\_

    a. .
    b. ?
    c. ,
    d. !

2. We saw many beautiful sights on our vacation\_\_\_\_ but we spent too many hours on the road.

    a. ,
    b. :
    c. ;
    d. .

**48      TABE® SKILL PRACTICE**

**3. She loved fresh vegetables at dinner _____ he wanted only meat on his dinner table.**

    a. ,
    b. :
    c. ;
    d. .

**4. Cautiously, he investigated the noise _____ but it was only the cat scratching the door.**

    a. !
    b. :
    c. ;
    d. .

**5. We packed a tent, several sleeping bags, a stove _____ and plenty of foods.**

    a. ,
    b. :
    c. ;
    d. .

**6. Choose the sentence below with the correct punctuation.**

    a. George wrecked John's car that was the end of their friendship.

    b. George wrecked John's car. that was the end of their friendship.

    c. George wrecked John's car; that was the end of their friendship.

    d. None of the above

# Practice Test Questions 1

**7. Choose the sentence below with the correct punctuation.**

    a. The dress was not Gina's favorite; however, she wore it to the dance.

    b. The dress was not Gina's favorite, however, she wore it to the dance.

    c. The dress was not Gina's favorite, however; she wore it to the dance.

    d. The dress was not Gina's favorite however, she wore it to the dance.

**8. Choose the sentence below with the correct punctuation.**

    a. Chris showed his dedication to golf in many ways, for example, he watched all the tournaments on television.

    b. Chris showed his dedication to golf in many ways; for example, he watched all the tournaments on television.

    c. Chris showed his dedication to golf in many ways, for example; he watched all the tournaments on television.

    d. Chris showed his dedication to golf in many ways for example he watched all the tournaments on television.

**9. Choose the sentence below with the correct punctuation.**

    a. There are many species of owls, the Great-Horned Owl, the Snowy Owl, and the Western Screech Owl, and the Barn Owl.

    b. There are many species of owls, the Great-Horned Owl: the Snowy Owl: and the Western Screech Owl, and the Barn Owl.

    c. There are many species of owls; the Great-Horned Owl, the Snowy Owl, and the Western Screech Owl, and the Barn Owl.

    d. There are many species of owls: the Great-Horned Owl, the Snowy Owl, the Western Screech Owl, and the Barn Owl.

**10. Choose the sentence below with the correct punctuation.**

a. In his most famous speech, Reverend King proclaimed: "I have a dream!"

b. In his most famous speech, Reverend King proclaimed; "I have a dream!"

c. In his most famous speech, Reverend King proclaimed. "I have a dream!"

d. In his most famous speech: Reverend King proclaimed, "I have a dream!"

**11. Choose the sentence with the correct punctuation and capitalization.**

a. "How often do you read the newspaper?" his father asked.

b. How often do you read the newspaper. His father asked.

c. "How often do you read the newspaper, his father asked?

d. How often do you read the newspaper his father asked.

**12. Choose the sentence with the correct punctuation and capitalization.**

a. The City of Miami is not the capital of Florida.

b. Tallahassee has been the capital of florida since 1,824.

c. Where can I find Californias best beaches?

d. My parents used to live in brooklyn, New York.

# Practice Test Questions 1

**13. Choose the sentence with the correct punctuation and capitalization.**

   a. The Wall street journal and New York times are popular newspapers.

   b. I read the Chicago Tribune every day.

   c. Mr Smith has the Weekend Newspaper delivered to his home.

   d. Usa Today is published by the Gannett Company.

**14. Choose the sentence with the correct punctuation and capitalization.**

   a. The ANB is the bank, the only bank, that I trust with my money.

   b. The ANB is the bank; The Only Bank; that I trust with my money.

   c. The ANB is the bank the only bank that I trust with my money.

   d. The ANB is the bank – the only bank that I trust with my money.

**15. Choose the sentence with the correct punctuation and capitalization.**

   a. John Legend performed "All of Me" at the 2014 Grammys.

   b. John Legend performed All of Me at the Grammys.

   c. John Legend performed – All of Me – at the Grammys.

   d. John Legend Performed "All of me at the 2014 Grammys."

**16. Combine the following two sentences into one sentence with the same meaning.**

**He writes poetry.**
**He plays sports.**

> a. He writes poetry as well as sports.
>
> b. He writes poetry instead of playing sports.
>
> c. He not only writes poetry, but also plays sports.
>
> d. He writes poetry to play sports.

**17. Combine the following two sentences into one sentence with the same meaning.**

**The student was punished.**
**The student was rude to the teacher.**

> a. The student was punished as a result of being rude to the teacher.
>
> b. Even if the student was rude to the teacher, he was punished.
>
> c. Because the student was punished, he was rude to the teacher.
>
> d. The student was rude to the teacher but he was punished.

**18. Combine the following two sentences into one sentence with the same meaning.**

**He failed his exam**
**He is quite lazy.**

> a. He is quite lazy after he failed his exam.
>
> b. He failed his exam because he is quite lazy.
>
> c. Although he failed his exam he is quite lazy.
>
> d. Only if he failed his exam he is quite lazy.

19. Combine the following two sentences into one sentence with the same meaning.

**Paolo will not be allowed to go.**
**Paolo has not completed his chores.**

   a. Despite Paolo not completing his chores, he will not be allowed to go.

   b. Paolo has not completed his chores, although he will not be allowed to go.

   c. So that Paolo has not completed his chores, he will not be allowed to go.

   d. If Paolo has not completed his chores, he will not be allowed to go.

20. Combine the following two sentences into one sentence with the same meaning.

**My mother picked up her car keys.**
**My mother plans to drive to the store.**

   a. My mother picked up her car keys as she plans to drive to the store.

   b. When my mother plans to drive to the store she pick up her car keys.

   c. Even if my mother picked up her car keys, she plans to drive to the store.

   d. My mother picked up her car keys but she plans to drive to the store.

# 54 TABE® SKILL PRACTICE

Directions: For questions 21 - 24 below, you are given a topic sentence. Choose the sentence which best develops the given topic sentence.

**21. Acquiring real estate is an important investment.**

a. Interest rates on mortgage are at an all-time low.

b. Older homes have a certain aesthetic appeal to mature buyers.

c. This decision should be made only after thorough research.

d. Banks usual don't give mortgages to unqualified individuals.

**22. Taking vacations together helps to strengthen family bonds.**

a. Many families choose to book their flights months in advance.

b. Travelling by plane is can be expensive and unsafe.

c. Members return home with a fresh perspective on life.

d. Children enjoy vacations because it's a time to have fun.

**23. Global economic imbalances have contributed to poverty.**

a. 75 percent of America's wealth is controlled by the richest ten percent.

b. Clean drinking water is scarce in some developing countries.

c. Many people in the poorest countries die from hunger daily.

d. Unemployment and illiteracy are on the rise globally.

## Practice Test Questions 1    55

**24. A job interview is a potential employee's chance to make a good impression.**

a. Managers sometimes fire employees because of misconduct.

b. A first degree is no longer enough to qualify for certain jobs.

c. Employers usually prefer interviewees with experience.

d. Interviewees are first judged by how they are dressed.

**25. Player performance and behavior affect attendance at NBA matches.**

a. Michael Jordan is the best basketball player of all time.

b. Disenchanted fans often stay away as a form of protest.

c. Though games are televised, the court side experience is better.

d. The NBA lays out strict rules that players must follow on court.

**Questions 26 - 30 refer to the following passage.**

**Read the passage below and look at the numbered, underlined phrases. Choose the answer that is written correctly for each underlined part.**

Insects, like humans, assimilate themselves into communities. Humans, as well as insects (26), divide labor among the individual members, with individuals or members carrying out unique roles, responsibilities or functions. Not all humans are equipped by (27) the same skills. Neither are all insects within the same community or colony. In some colonies the function of some insects are for reproduction (28), others carry out the day to day labor such as collecting food or constructing homes, and still others function as protectors or defenders, ensuring the overall safety of the community. Humans too have their assigned functions within their communities. There are construction workers which provide homes for the rest of the community to dwell in. There are farmers who produce the food to feed the community. There are police, soldiers and security guards that see about the safety of the community. Of course, in human communities, unlike among insects, there is significant overlap in functions. The human who gathers food in the field also builds the home and keeps it safe. However neither male humans nor most male insects, no matter how much they may desire it, are able to take on the reproductive role.

One difference over insect and human communities (29) is the principle of working together for the communal good. Among insect colonies, such as termites and ants, all efforts are united to achieve the community goal. Humans generally don't work together for the common goal, except it involves a job for which they are being paid.

Insects are innately programed to carry out their duties. From observations there is never a sense of being cheated or wanting to advance ahead of the colony into a role of superiority. Television shows may depict human character traits in insects but that's all a farce. Insects do not have the ability to develop those patterns of behavior. Perhaps its high time (30) humans really learn from insects.

**26. Choose the correct version.**

    a. Humans, moreover insects

    b. Humans, also as insects

    c. Humans, additional insects

    d. Correct as is.

**27. Choose the correct version.**

    a. humans are equipped with

    b. humans are equipped by

    c. humans are equipt with

    d. Correct as is.

# Practice Test Questions 1

**28. Choose the correct version.**

   a. the function of some insects were for reproduction
   b. the functions of some insects is for reproduction
   c. the function of some insect is for reproductions
   d. Correct as is.

**29. Choose the correct version.**

   a. difference among insect and human communities
   b. difference from insect and human communities
   c. difference between insect and human communities
   d. Correct as is.

**30. Choose the correct version.**

   a. Perhaps it's high time
   b. Perhaps it'll be high time
   c. Perhaps its' high time
   d. Correct as is.

**31. When Craig's dog was struck by a car, he rushed his pet to the _____.**

   a. Emergency room
   b. Doctor
   c. Veterinarian
   d. Podiatrist

**32. After she received her influenza vaccination, Nan thought that she was _____ to the common cold.**

   a. Immune
   b. Susceptible
   c. Vulnerable
   d. At risk

**33.** Paul's rose bushes were being destroyed by Japanese beetles, so he invested in a good _____.

   a. Fungicide
   b. Fertilizer
   c. Sprinkler
   d. Pesticide

**34.** The last time that the crops failed, the entire nation experienced months of _____.

   a. Famine
   b. Harvest
   c. Plentitude
   d. Disease

**35.** Because of a pituitary dysfunction, Karl lacked the necessary _____ to grow as tall as his father.

   a. Glands
   b. Hormones
   c. Vitamins
   d. Testosterone

**For questions 36 - 40, choose the word that best completes both sentences.**

**36.** He never agrees with his political party. He has a reputation as a _____.

Her reputation as a _____ often gets her into trouble.

   a. Maverick
   b. Conformist
   c. Insider
   d. None of the above

# PRACTICE TEST QUESTIONS 1

**37. With 8 kids, their house is always _____.**

**The 50% off sale was _____.**

    a. Noisy
    b. Orderly
    c. Pandemonium
    d. None of the above

**38. The water slowly _____ into the earth.**

**Don't worry it will _____ in a few minutes.**

    a. Degenerate
    b. Dissipate
    c. Scatter
    d. None of the above

**39. His skinny frame and _____ face scared me.**

**His eyes were sunken and his face was _____ .**

    a. Gaunt
    b. Straight
    c. Sallow
    d. None of the above

**40. The _____ was much more than I expected.**

**Your _____ will be paid at the end of the day.**

    a. Donation
    b. Remuneration
    c. Warning
    d. None of the above

**41. High performance cars like that require constant _____.**

    a. Maintainance

    b. Maintenace

    c. Maintanance

    d. Maintenance

**42. I didn't find it very _____.**

    a. Humoros

    b. Humouros

    c. Humorous

    d. Humorus

**43. She hasn't been here to my _____.**

    a. Knowlege

    b. Knowledge

    c. Knowlegde

    d. Knowlledge

**44. I never was very good at _____.**

    a. Mathematics

    b. Mathmatics

    c. Matematics

    d. Mathamatics

**45. I will look at it when I have some _____ time.**

    a. Leisuire

    b. Lesure

    c. Lesure

    d. Leisure

## Practice Test Questions 1

**46. Choose the phrase that is not spelled correctly.**

   a. sufficeint resources
   b. collectible coins
   c. inconvenient truth
   d. fourth revision

**47. Choose the phrase that is not spelled correctly.**

   a. gothic cemetery
   b. magicaley disappear
   c. broccoli and cheese
   d. baked potatoes

**48. Choose the phrase that is not spelled correctly.**

   a. heavy equipmment
   b. English grammar
   c. weird sounds
   d. high intelligence

**49. Choose the phrase that is not spelled correctly.**

   a. foreign accent
   b. minature house
   c. mischievous elves
   d. changeable weather

**50. Choose the phrase that is not spelled correctly.**

   a. turn of the millennium
   b. sharp scissors
   c. disatrous outcome
   d. glass ceiling

# Answer Key

## Section 1 – Reading

**1. A**
The correct answer because that fact is stated directly in the passage. The passage explains that Anne taught Helen to hear by allowing her to feel the vibrations in her throat.

**2. B**
We can infer that Anne is a patient teacher because she did not leave or lose her temper when Helen bit or hit her; she just kept trying to teach Helen. Choice B is incorrect because Anne taught Helen to read and talk. Choice C is incorrect because Anne could hear. She was partially blind, not deaf. Choice D is incorrect because it does not have to do with patience.

**3. A**
The passage states that it was hard for anyone but Anne to understand Helen when she spoke. Choice A is incorrect because the passage does not mention Helen spoke a foreign language. Choice C is incorrect because there is no mention of how quiet or loud Helen's voice was. Choice D is incorrect because we know from reading the passage that Helen did learn to speak.

**4. B**
This question tests the reader's summarization skills. The other choices A, B, and C focus on portions of the second paragraph that are too narrow and do not relate to the specific portion of text in question. The complexity of the sentence may mislead students into selecting one of these answers, but rearranging or restating the sentence will lead the reader to the correct answer. In addition, choice A makes an assumption that may or may not be true about the intentions of the company, choice B focuses on one product rather than the idea of the products, and choice C makes an assumption about women that may or may not be true and

# Practice Test Questions 1

is not supported by the text.

**5. D**
This question tests the reader's summarization skills. The question is asking very generally about the message of the passage, and the title, "Ways Characters Communicate in Theater," is one indication of that. The other choices A, B, and C are all directly from the text, and therefore readers may be inclined to select one of them, but are too specific to encapsulate the entirety of the passage and its message.

**6. B**
The paragraph on soliloquies mentions "To be or not to be," and it is from the context of that paragraph that readers may understand that because "To be or not to be" is a soliloquy, Hamlet will be introspective, or thoughtful, while delivering it. It is true that actors deliver soliloquies alone, and may be "solitary" (choice A), but "thoughtful" (choice B) is more true to the overall idea of the paragraph. Readers may choose C because drama and theater can be used interchangeably and the passage mentions that soliloquies are unique to theater (and therefore drama), but this answer is not specific enough to the paragraph in question. Readers may pick up on the theme of life and death and Hamlet's true intentions and select that he is "hopeless" (choice D), but those themes are not discussed either by this paragraph or passage, as a close textual reading and analysis confirms.

**7. C**
This question tests the reader's grammatical skills. Choice B seems logical, but parenthesis are actually considered to be a stronger break in a sentence than commas are, and along this line of thinking, actually disrupt the sentence more.

Choices A and D make comparisons between theater and film that are simply not made in the passage, and may or may not be true. This detail does clarify the statement that asides are most unique to theater by adding that it is not completely unique to theater, which may have been why the author didn't chose not to delete it and instead used parentheses to designate the detail's importance (choice C).

**8. A**
Low blood sugar occurs both in diabetics and healthy adults.

**9. B**
None of the statements are the author's opinion.

**10. A**
The author's purpose is the inform.

**11. A**
The only statement that is not a detail is, "A doctor can diagnosis this medical condition by asking the patient questions and testing."

**12. A**
This sentence is a recommendation.

**13. C**
Tips for a good night's sleep is the best alternative title for this article.

**14. B**
Mental activity is helpful for a good night's sleep is cannot be inferred from this article.

**15. A**
From the passage, one disadvantage of taking naps is they may keep you awake at night.

**16. C**
Based on the partial table of contents, you would find information about natural selection in the ecology section on page 110.

**17. C**
To be infamous means to be remembered for an evil or terrible action. Therefore, the word infamy means to remember a bad or terrible thing. Choice A is incorrect because being famous is not the same as being infamous. Choice B is incorrect because the attack on Pearl Harbor was not good. Choice D is incorrect because Pearl Harbor was not forgotten.

**18. C**
Each answer choice except choice C contains the name of at least one country that was not part of the AXIS powers.

# Practice Test Questions 1

**19. D**
It is stated in the passage. Choice A is not correct because there was no indication that Japan would attack San Diego. Choice B is incorrect because the attack on Pearl Harbor was a surprise. Choice C is incorrect because Roosevelt was not planning to attack Japan.

**20. C**
The passage clearly states that Japan planned a surprise attack. They chose that early time to catch the U.S. military off guard. Choice A is incorrect because the military does not sleep late. Choice B is incorrect because there is no law against bombing countries. Choice D is incorrect because it makes no sense.

**21. C**
This question tests the reader's vocabulary skills. The uses of the negatives "but" and "less," especially right next to each other, may confuse readers into answering with choices A or D, which list words that are antonyms to "militant." Readers may also be confused by the comparison of healthy people with what is being described as an overly healthy person--both people are good, but the reader may look for which one is "worse" in the comparison, and therefore stray toward the antonym words. The key to understanding the meaning of "militant" is to look at the root of the word; readers can then easily associate it with "military" and gain a sense of what the word signifies: defense (especially considered that the immune system defends the body). Choice C is correct over choice B because "militant" is an adjective, just as the words in choice C are, whereas the words in choice B are nouns.

**22. C**
This question tests the reader's understanding of function within writing. The other choices are details included surrounding the quoted text, and may therefore confuse the reader. A somewhat contradicts what is said earlier in the paragraph, which is that tests and treatments are improving, and probably doctors are along with them, but the paragraph doesn't actually mention doctors, and the subject of the question is the medicine. Choice B may seem correct to readers who aren't careful to understand that, while the author does mention the large number of people affected,

the author is touching on the realities of living with allergies rather than about the likelihood of curing all allergies. Similarly, while the author does mention the "balance" of the body, which is easily associated with "wholesome," the author is not really making an argument and especially is not making an extreme statement that allergy medicines should be outlawed. Again, because the article's tone is on living with allergies, choice C is an appropriate choice that fits with the title and content of the text.

**23. B**
This question tests the reader's inference skills. The text does not state who is doing the recommending, but the use of the "patients," as well as the general context of the passage, lends itself to the logical partner, "doctors," choice B. The author does mention the recommendation but doesn't present it as her own (i.e. "I recommend that"), so choice A may be eliminated. It may seem plausible that people with allergies (choice D) may recommend medicines or products to other people with allergies, but the text does not necessarily support this interaction taking place. Choice C may be selected because the EpiPen is specifically mentioned, but the use of the phrase "such as" when it is introduced is not limiting enough to assume the recommendation is coming from its creators.

**24. D**
This question tests the reader's global understanding of the text. Choice D includes the main topics of the three body paragraphs, and isn't too focused on a specific aspect or quote from the text, as the other questions are, giving a skewed summary of what the author intended. The reader may be drawn to choice B because of the title of the passage and the use of words like "better," but the message of the passage is larger and more general than this.

**25. B**
Reading the document posted to the Human Resources website is optional.

# Practice Test Questions 1    67

## Mathematics

**1. D**
75/1500 = 15/300 = 3/60 = 1/20

**2. B**
Estimate 215 X 65. First start with 200 X 50, which is 10,000, so the answer will be about 10,000. The only choice that is close is 13,500, choice B.

**3. B**

| Day | Number of Absent Students | Number of Present Students | % Attendance |
|---|---|---|---|
| Monday | 5 | 40 | 88.88% |
| Tuesday | 9 | 36 | 80.00% |
| Wednesday | 4 | 41 | 91.11% |
| Thursday | 10 | 35 | 77.77% |
| Friday | 6 | 39 | 86.66% |

88.88 + 80.00 + 91.11 + 77.77 + 86.66/5
424.42/5 = 84.88
Round up to 85%.

Percentage attendance will be 85%

**4. D**
First find a common denominator, 2/3 - 2/5 = 10 - 6 /15 = 4/15

**5. C**
0.27 + 0.33 = 0.60 and 0.60 = 60/100 = 3/5

**6. B**
(7 x 7 x 7 x 7 x 7) - (3 x 3 x 3 x 3 x 3) = 16,807 – 243 = 16,564

**7. B**
2/4 X 3/4 = 6/16, and reduced to the lowest terms = 3/8

**8. B**
4y + 24 = 3y + 30
4y − 3y = 30 - 24
y = 6

**9. B**
2/3 x 60 = 40 and 1/5 x 75 = 15, 40 + 15 = 55.

**10. A**
1/3 X 3/4 = 3/12 = 1/4

**11. D**
3.13 + 7.87 = 11 and 11 X 5 = 55

**12. A**
$5^6$

**13. C**
Exponential form is $9^3$ and standard from is 729

**14. B**
$(4)(3)^3$ = (4)(27) = 108

**15. B**
0.524/ 10 x 10 x 10 = 0.524/1000 = 0.000524

**16. C**
3x - 27 = 0
3x = 27
x = 9

**17. C**
First convert to decimal  7/11 = .63 and 5/7 = .714
2/3, choice C (.667) is the only choice between the two given numbers.

**18. B**
0.25 + 0.65 = 0.9 = 9/10

**19. C**
 389 + 454 = 843

# Practice Test Questions 1

**20. C**
9,177 + 7,204 = 16,381

**21. D**
2,199 + 5,832 = 8,031

**22. B**
8,390 - 5,239 = 3,151

**23. A**
643 - 587 = 56

**24. C**
3,406 - 2,767 = 639

**25. B**
149 × 7 = 1043

## Applied Mathematics

**1. D**
The formula for volume of a shape is L x W x H = 20 x 20 x 20 = 8,000 cm³

**2. D**
Let old salary = X, therefore $150 = x + 0.30x, 150 = 1x + 0.30x, 150 = 1.30x, x = 150/1.30 = 115.4

**3. C**
Cash = 51,300 + $75600 = $126,900. Building after one year = 80500 X 1.1 = $88550. Machinery after one year = 125000 X 0.8 = $100000. Total asset value = $315,450.

**4.**                                                                             **C**
If there are 5 friends and each drink costs $1.89, we can round up to $2 per drink and estimate the total cost at, 5 X $2 = $10.

The actual cost is 5 X $1.89 = $9.45.

**5. A**
At 100% efficiency 1 machine produces 1450/10 = 145 m of cloth.

At 95% efficiency, 4 machines produce (4 * 145 * 95)/100 = 551 m of cloth.

At 90% efficiency, 6 machines produce (6 * 145 * 90)/100 = 783 m of cloth.

Total cloth produced by all 10 machines = 551 + 783 = 1334 m

Since the information provided and the question are based on 8 hours, we did not need to use time to reach the answer.

**6. A**
The correct equation is X + 0.005xy.

**7. A**
The graph shows oil consumption peaked in 2011.

**8. D**
To find the total turnout in all three polling stations, we need to proportion the number of voters to the number of all registered voters.

Total number of voters = 945 + 860 + 1210 = 3015

Total number of registered voters = 1270 + 1050 + 1440 = 3760

Percentage turnout in all three polling stations = 3015•100/3760 = 80.19%

Check the answer, ound 80.19 to the nearest whole number: 80%

**9. B**
Total expenses = 5284.34 + $8,384.76 + $2,920.00 = 16589.10

Profit = revenue less expenses

$19,304.56 - $16,589.10 = $2,715.46

**10. D**
The formula for area is S (squared), and if the perimeter is 100, each side will be 25, the the area is 25 squared.

# Practice Test Questions 1    71

**11. B**
40% of 8.50 = 8.5 X .4 = $3.40.  Including tips, $3.40 + 1.30 = $4.70

**12. D**
Taking Mr. Jones's total to calculate the price of an adult ticket, 38.5/7 = 5.5.  Mr. Jones bought 9 adult tickets for a cost of 9 X 5.5 = $49.50.

Total cost was 67, so to calculate the cost of children's ticket, 67 - 49.5 = 17.5.  17.5/5 = $3.50

**13. C**
Equilateral triangle with 9 cm. sides
Perimeter = 9 + 9 + 9 = 27 cm.

**14. D**
Perimeter of triangle ABC is asked.
Perimeter of a triangle = sum of three sides.

Here, Perimeter of △ABC = |AC| + |CB| + |AB|.

Since the triangle is located in the middle of two adjacent and identical rectangles, we find the side lengths using these rectangles:

|AB| = 6 + 6 = 12 cm

|CB| = 8.5 cm

|AC| = |CB| = 8.5 cm

Perimeter = |AC| + |CB| + |AB| = 8.5 + 8.5 + 12 = 29 cm

**15. B**
She spent 15% - 100% - 15% = 85%

**16. D**
Formula for volume of a shape is L x W x H = 10 x 8 x 10 = 800 cm$^3$

**17. B**
This is a compound interest problem.  Calculate the interest earned in the first year and then use that total for the second year calculation.

In the first year, 5000 X .04 = 200
In the second year, 5200 X .04 = 208
Total at the end of the second year = $5408

**18. B**
The distribution is at three different rates and amounts:

$6.4 per 20 kilograms to 15 shops ... 20 * 15 = 300 kilograms distributed

$3.4 per 10 kilograms to 12 shops ... 10 * 12 = 120 kilograms distributed

550 - (300 + 120) = 550 - 420 = 130 kilograms left. This amount is distributed by 5 kilogram portions. So, this means that there are 130/5 = 26 shops.

$1.8 per 130 kilograms.

We need to find the amount he earned overall these distributions.

$6.4 per 20 kilograms : 6.4 * 15 = $96 for 300 kilograms

$3.4 per 10 kilograms : 3.4 * 12 = $40.8 for 120 kilograms

$1.8 per 5 kilograms : 1.8 * 26 = $46.8 for 130 kilograms

So, he earned 96 + 40.8 + 46.8 = $ 183.6

The total distribution cost is given as $10

The profit is found by: Money earned - money spent ... It is important to remember that he bought 550 kilograms of potatoes for $165 at the beginning:

Profit = 183.6 - 10 - 165 = $8.6

**19. D**
The distance covered by the car = 60 X 3.5 = 210 km. Time required by the motorbike = 210/40 = 5.25 hr.

# Practice Test Questions 1    73

**20. D**
The number is 51.738. The last digit is greater than 5, so it is removed and 1 is added to the next number to the left. Answer = 51.74.

**21. C**
The ratio between gold, silver and bronze coins is 2:6:12. Bring to the lowest terms by dividing each element in the original ratio by 2 gives 1:3:6.

**22. B**
The line is pointing towards numbers less than 1. The equation is therefore, X < 1.

**23. A**
The line is pointing towards numbers greater than 2. The equation is therefore, X < 2.

**24. C**
The decimal point moves 9 spaces right to be placed after 7, which is the first non-zero number. Thus $7.892 \times 10^9$

**25. D**
Each time the * and + alternate, either singly or doubles.

# English

**1. D**
Use an exclamation mark after an imperative sentence if the command is urgent and forceful.

**2. A**
A comma is used before the conjunction to separate two independent clauses in a compound sentence.

**3. C**
A semicolon is also used to join two clauses that present a direct contrast. In this question, the sentence has two extremes in a similar situation. Notice that even when the two clauses present a contrast, the subjects of the two clauses are similar.

**4. C**
A semi colon may also be used to prevent confusion. The other obvious choice is this sentence would be a comma, but it isn't a choice.

**5. A**
A comma is used to separate three or more words, phrases or clauses in a series.

**6. C**
The semicolon links independent clauses.

**7. A**
The semicolon links independent clauses with a conjunction (However).

**8. B**
The semicolon links independent clauses.

**9. D**
A colon informs the reader that what follows the mark proves, explains, or lists elements of what preceded the mark.

**10. A**
A colon informs the reader that what follows the mark proves, explains, or lists elements of what preceded the mark.

**11. A**
Choice A is the only choice that includes quotation marks around the quoted speech and a question mark.

**12. A**
In choice A, "city" is capitalized because it is used in the phrase, "City of Miami." "Florida" in this sentence is also correctly capitalized. Choice B does not capitalize "Florida." Choice C omits an apostrophe in "California's best beaches." Choice D does not capitalize "Brooklyn."

**13. B**
Choice A has incorrect capitalization of "Wall Street Journal." The names of publications are capitalized. Choice C

# Practice Test Questions 1

incorrect capitalizes "Weekend Newspaper." Choice D incorrectly capitalizes "USA Today."

**14. D**
Choice A uses commas incorrectly. Choice B uses both commas and capitalization incorrectly, and choice D uses a dash where it is not required.

**15. A**
Choice A correctly capitalizes the singers name, includes the name of the song in quotes, as well as capitalizes "Grammys." Choice B does not include the name of the song in quotes. Choice C incorrectly uses dashes, and choice D incorrectly uses quotation marks.

**16. C**
**17. A**
**18. B**
**19. D**
**20. A**
**21. C**
**22. C**
**23. C**
**24. D**
**25. B**
**26. D**
The sentence is correct. The other choices add an additional and unnecessary comma.

**27. A**
"Equipt" is incorrect - the correct form is "equipped with."

**28. D**
The phrase, "function of some insects" is singular, so "is" is correct.

**29. C**
The correct usage for comparing two things is "difference between."

**30. A**
Choice A uses the contraction "it's" correctly.

## Vocabulary

**31. C**
**Veterinarian:** a person qualified to treat diseased or injured animals.

**32. A**
**Immune:** resistant to a particular virus or toxin.

**33. D**
**Pesticide:** a substance used for destroying insects or other organisms harmful to cultivated plants or to animals.

**34. A**
**Famine:** extreme scarcity of food.

**35. B**
**Hormones:** a regulatory substance produced in an organism and transported in tissue fluids such as blood or sap to stimulate specific cells or tissues into action.

**36. A**
**Maverick:** Showing independence in thoughts or actions.

**37. C**
**Pandemonium:** wild and noisy disorder or confusion; uproar.

**38. B**
**Dissipate:** disperse or scatter.

**39. A**
**Gaunt:** lean and haggard, esp. because of suffering, hunger, or age.

**40. B**
**Remuneration:** A payment for work done; wages, salary.

# Practice Test Questions 1

## Spelling

**41. D**
Maintenance is the correct spelling.

**42. C**
Humorous is the correct spelling.

**43. B**
Knowledge is the correct spelling.

**44. A**
Mathematics is the correct spelling.

**45. D**
Leisure is the correct spelling.

**46. A**
Sufficeint is incorrect. The correct spelling is sufficient.

**47. B**
Magicaley is incorrect. The correct spelling is magically.

**48. A**
Equipmment is incorrect. The correct spelling is equipment.

**49. B**
Minature is incorrect. The correct spelling is miniature.

**50. C**
Disatrous is incorrect. The correct spelling is disastrous.

# Practice Test Questions Set 2

The practice test portion presents questions that are representative of the type of question you should expect to find on the TABE®. However, they are not intended to match exactly what is on the TABE®.

For the best results, take this Practice Test as if it were the real exam. Set aside time when you will not be disturbed, and a location that is quiet and free of distractions. Read the instructions carefully, read each question carefully, and answer to the best of your ability.

Use the bubble answer sheets provided. When you have completed the Practice Test, check your answer against the Answer Key and read the explanation provided.

# Practice Test Questions 2

**Reading**

|    | A | B | C | D | E |    | A | B | C | D | E |
|----|---|---|---|---|---|----|---|---|---|---|---|
| 1  | ○ | ○ | ○ | ○ | ○ | 21 | ○ | ○ | ○ | ○ | ○ |
| 2  | ○ | ○ | ○ | ○ | ○ | 22 | ○ | ○ | ○ | ○ | ○ |
| 3  | ○ | ○ | ○ | ○ | ○ | 23 | ○ | ○ | ○ | ○ | ○ |
| 4  | ○ | ○ | ○ | ○ | ○ | 24 | ○ | ○ | ○ | ○ | ○ |
| 5  | ○ | ○ | ○ | ○ | ○ | 25 | ○ | ○ | ○ | ○ | ○ |
| 6  | ○ | ○ | ○ | ○ | ○ |    |   |   |   |   |   |
| 7  | ○ | ○ | ○ | ○ | ○ |    |   |   |   |   |   |
| 8  | ○ | ○ | ○ | ○ | ○ |    |   |   |   |   |   |
| 9  | ○ | ○ | ○ | ○ | ○ |    |   |   |   |   |   |
| 10 | ○ | ○ | ○ | ○ | ○ |    |   |   |   |   |   |
| 11 | ○ | ○ | ○ | ○ | ○ |    |   |   |   |   |   |
| 12 | ○ | ○ | ○ | ○ | ○ |    |   |   |   |   |   |
| 13 | ○ | ○ | ○ | ○ | ○ |    |   |   |   |   |   |
| 14 | ○ | ○ | ○ | ○ | ○ |    |   |   |   |   |   |
| 15 | ○ | ○ | ○ | ○ | ○ |    |   |   |   |   |   |
| 16 | ○ | ○ | ○ | ○ | ○ |    |   |   |   |   |   |
| 17 | ○ | ○ | ○ | ○ | ○ |    |   |   |   |   |   |
| 18 | ○ | ○ | ○ | ○ | ○ |    |   |   |   |   |   |
| 19 | ○ | ○ | ○ | ○ | ○ |    |   |   |   |   |   |
| 20 | ○ | ○ | ○ | ○ | ○ |    |   |   |   |   |   |

## Computational Mathematics

|   | A | B | C | D | E |   |   | A | B | C | D | E |
|---|---|---|---|---|---|---|---|---|---|---|---|---|
| 1 | ○ | ○ | ○ | ○ | ○ |   | 21 | ○ | ○ | ○ | ○ | ○ |
| 2 | ○ | ○ | ○ | ○ | ○ |   | 22 | ○ | ○ | ○ | ○ | ○ |
| 3 | ○ | ○ | ○ | ○ | ○ |   | 23 | ○ | ○ | ○ | ○ | ○ |
| 4 | ○ | ○ | ○ | ○ | ○ |   | 24 | ○ | ○ | ○ | ○ | ○ |
| 5 | ○ | ○ | ○ | ○ | ○ |   | 25 | ○ | ○ | ○ | ○ | ○ |
| 6 | ○ | ○ | ○ | ○ | ○ |   |   |   |   |   |   |   |
| 7 | ○ | ○ | ○ | ○ | ○ |   |   |   |   |   |   |   |
| 8 | ○ | ○ | ○ | ○ | ○ |   |   |   |   |   |   |   |
| 9 | ○ | ○ | ○ | ○ | ○ |   |   |   |   |   |   |   |
| 10 | ○ | ○ | ○ | ○ | ○ |   |   |   |   |   |   |   |
| 11 | ○ | ○ | ○ | ○ | ○ |   |   |   |   |   |   |   |
| 12 | ○ | ○ | ○ | ○ | ○ |   |   |   |   |   |   |   |
| 13 | ○ | ○ | ○ | ○ | ○ |   |   |   |   |   |   |   |
| 14 | ○ | ○ | ○ | ○ | ○ |   |   |   |   |   |   |   |
| 15 | ○ | ○ | ○ | ○ | ○ |   |   |   |   |   |   |   |
| 16 | ○ | ○ | ○ | ○ | ○ |   |   |   |   |   |   |   |
| 17 | ○ | ○ | ○ | ○ | ○ |   |   |   |   |   |   |   |
| 18 | ○ | ○ | ○ | ○ | ○ |   |   |   |   |   |   |   |
| 19 | ○ | ○ | ○ | ○ | ○ |   |   |   |   |   |   |   |
| 20 | ○ | ○ | ○ | ○ | ○ |   |   |   |   |   |   |   |

# Practice Test Questions 2

## Applied Mathematics

|    | A | B | C | D | E |    | A | B | C | D | E |
|----|---|---|---|---|---|----|---|---|---|---|---|
| 1  | ○ | ○ | ○ | ○ | ○ | 21 | ○ | ○ | ○ | ○ | ○ |
| 2  | ○ | ○ | ○ | ○ | ○ | 22 | ○ | ○ | ○ | ○ | ○ |
| 3  | ○ | ○ | ○ | ○ | ○ | 23 | ○ | ○ | ○ | ○ | ○ |
| 4  | ○ | ○ | ○ | ○ | ○ | 24 | ○ | ○ | ○ | ○ | ○ |
| 5  | ○ | ○ | ○ | ○ | ○ | 25 | ○ | ○ | ○ | ○ | ○ |
| 6  | ○ | ○ | ○ | ○ | ○ |    |   |   |   |   |   |
| 7  | ○ | ○ | ○ | ○ | ○ |    |   |   |   |   |   |
| 8  | ○ | ○ | ○ | ○ | ○ |    |   |   |   |   |   |
| 9  | ○ | ○ | ○ | ○ | ○ |    |   |   |   |   |   |
| 10 | ○ | ○ | ○ | ○ | ○ |    |   |   |   |   |   |
| 11 | ○ | ○ | ○ | ○ | ○ |    |   |   |   |   |   |
| 12 | ○ | ○ | ○ | ○ | ○ |    |   |   |   |   |   |
| 13 | ○ | ○ | ○ | ○ | ○ |    |   |   |   |   |   |
| 14 | ○ | ○ | ○ | ○ | ○ |    |   |   |   |   |   |
| 15 | ○ | ○ | ○ | ○ | ○ |    |   |   |   |   |   |
| 16 | ○ | ○ | ○ | ○ | ○ |    |   |   |   |   |   |
| 17 | ○ | ○ | ○ | ○ | ○ |    |   |   |   |   |   |
| 18 | ○ | ○ | ○ | ○ | ○ |    |   |   |   |   |   |
| 19 | ○ | ○ | ○ | ○ | ○ |    |   |   |   |   |   |
| 20 | ○ | ○ | ○ | ○ | ○ |    |   |   |   |   |   |

## Language

|    | A | B | C | D | E |    | A | B | C | D | E |
|----|---|---|---|---|---|----|---|---|---|---|---|
| 1  | ○ | ○ | ○ | ○ | ○ | 21 | ○ | ○ | ○ | ○ | ○ |
| 2  | ○ | ○ | ○ | ○ | ○ | 22 | ○ | ○ | ○ | ○ | ○ |
| 3  | ○ | ○ | ○ | ○ | ○ | 23 | ○ | ○ | ○ | ○ | ○ |
| 4  | ○ | ○ | ○ | ○ | ○ | 24 | ○ | ○ | ○ | ○ | ○ |
| 5  | ○ | ○ | ○ | ○ | ○ | 25 | ○ | ○ | ○ | ○ | ○ |
| 6  | ○ | ○ | ○ | ○ | ○ | 26 | ○ | ○ | ○ | ○ | ○ |
| 7  | ○ | ○ | ○ | ○ | ○ | 27 | ○ | ○ | ○ | ○ | ○ |
| 8  | ○ | ○ | ○ | ○ | ○ | 28 | ○ | ○ | ○ | ○ | ○ |
| 9  | ○ | ○ | ○ | ○ | ○ | 29 | ○ | ○ | ○ | ○ | ○ |
| 10 | ○ | ○ | ○ | ○ | ○ | 30 | ○ | ○ | ○ | ○ | ○ |
| 11 | ○ | ○ | ○ | ○ | ○ | 31 | ○ | ○ | ○ | ○ | ○ |
| 12 | ○ | ○ | ○ | ○ | ○ | 32 | ○ | ○ | ○ | ○ | ○ |
| 13 | ○ | ○ | ○ | ○ | ○ | 33 | ○ | ○ | ○ | ○ | ○ |
| 14 | ○ | ○ | ○ | ○ | ○ | 34 | ○ | ○ | ○ | ○ | ○ |
| 15 | ○ | ○ | ○ | ○ | ○ | 35 | ○ | ○ | ○ | ○ | ○ |
| 16 | ○ | ○ | ○ | ○ | ○ | 36 | ○ | ○ | ○ | ○ | ○ |
| 17 | ○ | ○ | ○ | ○ | ○ | 37 | ○ | ○ | ○ | ○ | ○ |
| 18 | ○ | ○ | ○ | ○ | ○ | 38 | ○ | ○ | ○ | ○ | ○ |
| 19 | ○ | ○ | ○ | ○ | ○ | 39 | ○ | ○ | ○ | ○ | ○ |
| 20 | ○ | ○ | ○ | ○ | ○ | 40 | ○ | ○ | ○ | ○ | ○ |

# Reading and Language Arts

**Questions 1 - 4 refer to the following passage.**

**Passage 1 - The Crusades**

In 1095 Pope Urban II proclaimed the First Crusade with the intent and stated goal to restore Christian access to holy places in and around Jerusalem. Over the next 200 years there were 6 major crusades and numerous minor crusades in the fight for control of the "Holy Land." Historians are divided on the real purpose of the Crusades, some believing that it was part of a purely defensive war against Islamic conquest; some see them as part of a long-running conflict at the frontiers of Europe; and others see them as confident, aggressive, papal-led expansion attempts by Western Christendom. The impact of the crusades was profound, and judgment of the Crusaders ranges from laudatory to highly critical. However, all agree that the Crusades and wars waged during those crusades were brutal and often bloody. Several hundred thousand Roman Catholic Christians joined the Crusades, they were Christians from all over Europe.

Europe at the time was under the Feudal System, so while the Crusaders made vows to the Church they also were beholden to their Feudal Lords. This led to the Crusaders not only fighting the Saracen, the commonly used word for Muslim at the time, but also each other for power and economic gain in the Holy Land. This infighting between the Crusaders is why many historians hold the view that the Crusades were simply a front for Europe to invade the Holy Land for economic gain in the name of the Church. Another factor contributing to this theory is that while the army of crusaders marched towards Jerusalem they pillaged the land as they went. The church and feudal Lords vowing to return the land to its original beauty, and inhabitants, this rarely happened though as the Lords often kept the land for themselves. A full 800 years after the Crusades, Pope John Paul II expressed his sorrow for the massacre of innocent people and the lasting damage the Medieval church caused in that area of the World.

# TABE® SKILL PRACTICE

**1. What is the tone of this article?**

    a. Subjective

    b. Objective

    c. Persuasive

    d. None of the Above

**2. What can all historians agree on concerning the Crusades?**

    a. It achieved great things

    b. It stabilized the Holy Land

    c. It was bloody and brutal

    d. It helped defend Europe from the Byzantine Empire

**3. What impact did the feudal system have on the Crusades?**

    a. It unified the Crusaders

    b. It helped gather volunteers

    c. It had no effect on the Crusades

    d. It led to infighting, causing more damage than good

**4. What does Saracen mean?**

    a. Muslim

    b. Christian

    c. Knight

    d. Holy Land

## Practice Test Questions 2    85

Questions 5 - 8 refer to the following passage.

**ABC Electric Warranty**

ABC Electric Company warrants that its products are free from defects in material and workmanship. Subject to the conditions and limitations set forth below, ABC Electric will, at its option, either repair or replace any part of its products that prove defective due to improper workmanship or materials.

This limited warranty does not cover any damage to the product from improper installation, accident, abuse, misuse, natural disaster, insufficient or excessive electrical supply, abnormal mechanical or environmental conditions, or any unauthorized disassembly, repair, or modification.

This limited warranty also does not apply to any product on which the original identification information has been altered, or removed, has not been handled or packaged correctly, or has been sold as second-hand.

This limited warranty covers only repair, replacement, refund or credit for defective ABC Electric products, as provided above.

**5. I tried to repair my ABC Electric blender, but could not, so can I get it repaired under this warranty?**

    a.  Yes, the warranty still covers the blender

    b.  No, the warranty does not cover the blender

    c.  Uncertain. ABC Electric may or may not cover repairs under this warranty

6. My ABC Electric fan is not working. Will ABC Electric provide a new one or repair this one?

    a. ABC Electric will repair my fan

    b. ABC Electric will replace my fan

    c. ABC Electric could either replace or repair my fan can request either a replacement or a repair.

7. My stove was damaged in a flood. Does this warranty cover my stove?

    a. Yes, it is covered.

    b. No, it is not covered.

    c. It may or may not be covered.

    d. ABC Electric will decide if it is covered

8. Which of the following is an example of improper workmanship?

    a. Missing parts

    b. Defective parts

    c. Scratches on the front

    d. None of the above

Questions 9 – 12 refer to the following passage.

**Passage 2 - Women and Advertising**

Only in the last few generations have media messages been so widespread and so readily seen, heard, and read by so many people. Advertising is an important part of both selling and buying anything from soap to cereal to jeans. For whatever reason, more consumers are women than are men. Media message are subtle but powerful, and more attention has been paid lately to how these message affect women. Of all the products that women buy, makeup, clothes, and other stylistic or cosmetic products are among the most popular. This means that companies focus their advertising on women, promising them that their product will make her feel, look, or smell better than the next company's product will. This competition has resulted in advertising that is more and more ideal and less and less possible for everyday women. However, because women do look to these ideals and the products they represent as how they can potentially become, many women have developed unhealthy attitudes about themselves when they have failed to become those ideals.

In recent years, more companies have tried to change advertisements to be healthier for women. This includes featuring models of more sizes and addressing a huge outcry against unfair tools such as airbrushing and photo editing. There is debate about what the right balance between real and ideal is, because fashion is also considered art and some changes are made to purposefully elevate fashionable products and signify that they are creative, innovative, and the work of individual people. Artists want their freedom protected as much as women do, and advertising agencies are often caught in the middle.

Some claim that the companies who make these changes are not doing enough. Many people worry that there are still not enough models of different sizes and different ethnicities. Some people claim that companies use this healthier type of advertisement not for the good of women, but because they would like to sell products to the women who are looking for these kinds of messages. This is also a hard balance to find: companies do need to make money, and women do need to feel respected.

While the focus of this change has been on women, advertising can also affect men, and this change will hopefully be a lesson on media for all consumers.

**9. The second paragraph states that advertising focuses on women**

   a. to shape what the ideal should be

   b. because women buy makeup

   c. because women are easily persuaded

   d. because of the types of products that women buy

**10. According to the passage, fashion artists and female consumers are at odds because**

   a. there is a debate going on and disagreement drives people apart

   b. both of them are trying to protect their freedom to do something

   c. artists want to elevate their products above the reach of women

   d. women are creative, innovative, individual people

**11. The author uses the phrase "for whatever reason" in this passage to**

   a. keep the focus of the paragraph on media messages and not on the differences between men and women

   b. show that the reason for this is unimportant

   c. argue that it is stupid that more women are consumers than men

   d. show that he or she is tired of talking about why media messages are important

**12. This passage suggests that**

   a. advertising companies are still working on making their messages better

   b. all advertising companies seek to be more approachable for women

   c. women are only buying from companies that respect them

   d. artists could stop producing fashionable products if they feel bullied

## Practice Test Questions 2

**Questions 13 - 16 refer to the following passage.**

### FDR, the Treaty of Versailles, and the Fourteen Points

At the conclusion of World War I, those who had won the war and those who were forced to admit defeat welcomed the end of the war and expected that a peace treaty would be signed. The American president, Franklin D. Roosevelt, played an important part in proposing what the agreements should be and did so through his Fourteen Points.
World War I had begun in 1914 when an Austrian archduke was assassinated, leading to a domino effect that pulled the world's most powerful countries into war on a large scale. The war catalyzed the creation and use of deadly weapons that had not previously existed, resulting in a great loss of soldiers on both sides of the fighting. More than 9 million soldiers were killed.

The United States agreed to enter the war right before it ended, and many believed that its decision to become finally involved brought on the end of the war. FDR made it very clear that the U.S. was entering the war for moral reasons and had an agenda focused on world peace. The Fourteen Points were individual goals and ideas (focused on peace, free trade, open communication, and self reliance) that FDR wanted the power nations to strive for now that the war had concluded. He was optimistic and had many ideas about what could be accomplished through and during the post-war peace. However, FDR's fourteen points were poorly received when he presented them to the leaders of other world powers, many of whom wanted only to help their own countries and to punish the Germans for fueling the war, and they fell by the wayside. World War II was imminent, for Germany lost everything.

Some historians believe that the other leaders who participated in the Treaty of Versailles weren't receptive to the Fourteen Points because World War I was fought almost entirely on European soil, and the United States lost much less than did the other powers. FDR was in a unique position to determine the fate of the war, but doing it on his own terms did not help accomplish his goals. This is only one historical example of how the United State has tried to use its power as an important country, but found itself limited because of geological or ideological factors.

**13. The main idea of this passage is that**

    a. World War I was unfair because no fighting took place in America

    b. World War II happened because of the Treaty of Versailles

    c. the power the United States has to help other countries also prevents it from helping other countries

    d. Franklin D. Roosevelt was one of the United States' smartest presidents

**14. According to the second paragraph, World War I started because**

    a. an archduke was assassinated

    b. weapons that were more deadly had been developed

    c. a domino effect of allies agreeing to help each other

    d. the world's most powerful countries were large

**15. The author includes the detail that 9 million soldiers were killed**

    a. to demonstrate why European leaders were hesitant to accept peace

    b. to show the reader the dangers of deadly weapons

    c. to make the reader think about which countries lost the most soldiers

    d. to demonstrate why World War II was imminent

**16. According to this passage, the word catalyzed means**

a. analyzed
b. sped up
c. invented
d. funded

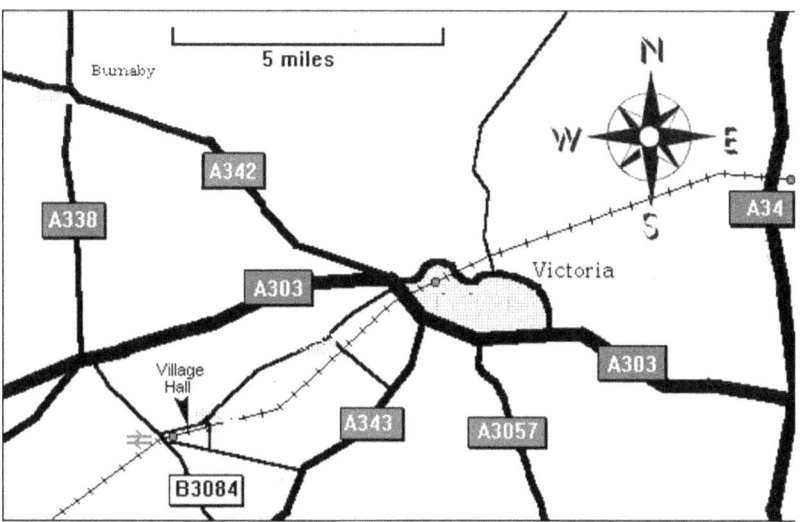

**17. Approximately how far is Victoria to Burnaby?**

a. About 10 miles
b. About 5 miles
c. About 15 miles
d. About 20 miles

**18. How is the Village Hall from Victoria?**

a. About 10 miles
b. About 5 miles
c. About 15 miles
d. About 20 miles

Questions 19 - 22 refer to the following passage.

**Chocolate Chip Cookies**

3/4 cup sugar
3/4 cup packed brown sugar
1 cup butter, softened
2 large eggs, beaten
1 teaspoon vanilla extract
2 1/4 cups all-purpose flour
1 teaspoon baking soda
3/4 teaspoon salt
2 cups semisweet chocolate chips
If desired, 1 cup chopped pecans, or chopped walnuts.
Preheat oven to 375 degrees.

Mix sugar, brown sugar, butter, vanilla and eggs in a large bowl. Stir in flour, baking soda, and salt. The dough will be very stiff.

Stir in chocolate chips by hand with a sturdy wooden spoon. Add the pecans, or other nuts, if desired. Stir until the chocolate chips and nuts are evenly dispersed.

Drop dough by rounded tablespoonfuls 2 inches apart onto a cookie sheet.

Bake 8 to 10 minutes or until light brown. Cookies may look underdone, but they will finish cooking after you take them out of the oven.

**19. What is the correct order for adding these ingredients?**

   a. Brown sugar, baking soda, chocolate chips
   b. Baking soda, brown sugar, chocolate chips
   c. Chocolate chips, baking soda, brown sugar
   d. Baking soda, chocolate chips, brown sugar

# Practice Test Questions 2       93

**20. What does sturdy mean?**

   a. Long
   b. Strong
   c. Short
   d. Wide


**21. What does disperse mean?**

   a. Scatter
   b. To form a ball
   c. To stir
   d. To beat


**22. When can you stop stirring the nuts?**

   a. When the cookies are cooked.
   b. When the nuts are evenly distributed.
   c. When the nuts are added.
   d. After the chocolate chips are added.


**Questions 23 - 26 refer to the following passage.**


**Passage 5 - Frankenstein**

Great God! What a scene has just taken place! I am yet dizzy with the remembrance of it. I hardly know whether I shall have the power to detail it; yet the tale which I have recorded would be incomplete without this final and wonderful catastrophe. I entered the cabin where lay the remains of my ill-fated and admirable friend. Over him hung a form which I cannot find words to describe—gigantic in stature, yet uncouth and distorted in its proportions. As he hung over the coffin, his face was concealed by long locks of ragged hair; but one vast hand was extended, in color and apparent texture like that of a mummy. When he heard the sound of my approach, he ceased to utter exclamations of grief and horror and sprung towards the window. Never did I behold a vision so horrible as his face, of such loathsome yet appalling hideousness. I shut my eyes involuntarily and endeavored to recollect what were my duties with regard to this destroyer. I called on him to stay.

He paused, looking on me with wonder, and again turning towards the lifeless form of his creator, he seemed to forget my presence, and every feature and gesture seemed instigated by the wildest rage of some uncontrollable passion.

"That is also my victim!" he exclaimed. "In his murder my crimes are consummated; the miserable series of my being is wound to its close! Oh, Frankenstein! Generous and self-devoted being! What does it avail that I now ask thee to pardon me? I, who irretrievably destroyed thee by destroying all thou lovedst. Alas! He is cold, he cannot answer me."

His voice seemed suffocated, and my first impulses, which had suggested to me the duty of obeying the dying request of my friend in destroying his enemy, were now suspended by a mixture of curiosity and compassion. I approached this tremendous being; I dared not again raise my eyes to his face, there was something so scaring and unearthly in his ugliness. I attempted to speak, but the words died away on my lips. The monster continued to utter wild and incoherent self-reproaches. At length I gathered resolution to address him in a pause of the tempest of his passion.

"Your repentance," I said, "is now superfluous. If you had listened to the voice of conscience and heeded the stings of remorse before you had urged your diabolical vengeance to this extremity, Frankenstein would yet have lived." [7]

**23. Who is the "ill-fated and admirable friend" who is lying in the coffin?**

    a. Frankenstein's monster

    b. Frankenstein

    c. Mary Shelley

    d. Unknown

# Practice Test Questions 2

**24. Why is the speaker 'suspended" from following through on his duty to destroy the monster?**

    a. The way the monster looks

    b. The monster's remorse

    c. Curiosity and compassion

    d. Fear the monster might kill him too

**25. How does Frankenstein's monster destroy Frankenstein?**

    a. By killing Frankenstein

    b. By letting himself be the monster everyone sees him as

    c. By destroying everything Frankenstein loved

    d. All of the above

## Computational Mathematics

**1. 8974 – 8256 =**

    a. 715

    b. 716

    c. 718

    d. 715

**2. 4404 / 8 =**

    a. 550.5

    b. 550

    c. 505

    d. 555

3. 274 * 139 =

    a. 38006
    b. 38860
    c. 38060
    d. 38086

4. 3567 + 99 =

    a. 3066
    b. 3666
    c. 3606
    d. 4666

5. Translate the following into an equation:

2 plus a number divided by 7.

    a. (2 + X)/7
    b. (7 + X)/2
    c. (2 + 7)/X
    d. 2/(7 + X)

6. 60 is 75% of x. Solve for x.

    a. 80
    b. 90
    c. 75
    d. 70

7. Express 71/1000 as a decimal.

    a. .71
    b. .0071
    c. .071
    d. 7.1

8. .33 × .59 =

   a. .1947
   b. 1.95
   c. .0197
   d. .1817

9. 7x − 9 = 47. Solve for x.

   a. 8
   b. 7
   c. 9
   d. 6

10. What number is in the ten thousandths place in 1.7389

    a. 1
    b. 8
    c. 9
    d. 3

11. .87 - .48 =

    a. .39
    b. .49
    c. .41
    d. .37

12. Which is the equivalent decimal number for forty nine thousandths?

    a. .49
    b. .0049
    c. .049
    d. 4.9

13. Which of the following is not a fraction equivalent to 3/4?

   a. 6/8
   b. 9/12
   c. 12/18
   d. 21/28

14. Which one of the following is greater than a third?

   a. 84/231
   b. 6/35
   c. 3/22
   d. b and c

15. Which of the following numbers is the greatest?

   a. 1
   b. $\sqrt{2}$
   c. 3/2
   d. 4/3

16. 2b + 9b − 5b = 0

   a. 3b
   b. 6b
   c. 4b
   d. 8b

17. 4.7 + .9 + .01 =

   a. 5.5
   b. 6.51
   c. 5.61
   d. 5.7

## Practice Test Questions 2

**18.** 60% of x is 12. Solve for x.

    a. 18
    b. 15
    c. 25
    d. 20

**19.** .84 ÷ .7 =

    a. .12
    b. 12
    c. .012
    d. 1.2

**20.** 4120 − 3216 =

    a. 903
    b. 804
    c. 904
    d. 1904

**21.** 2417 + 1004 =

    a. 3401
    b. 4321
    c. 3402
    d. 3421

**22.** Simplify 0.12 + 1 2/5 − 1 3/5

    a. 1 1/25
    b. -2/25
    c. 1 2/5
    d. 2 3/5

# 100     TABE® SKILL PRACTICE

23. What is the difference between 700,653 and 70,099?

    a. 4607854
    b. 5460
    c. 700765
    d. 630,554

24. Simplify 0.25 + 1/3 + 2/3

    a. 1 1/4
    b. 2 1/4
    c. 1 1/3
    d. 2 1/4

25. Add 10% of 300 to 50% of 20

    a. 50
    b. 40
    c. 60
    d. 45

# Applied Mathematics

1. If a train travels at 72 kilometers per hour, how far will it travel in 12 seconds?

    a. 200m
    b. 220m
    c. 240m
    d. 260m

# PRACTICE TEST QUESTIONS 2

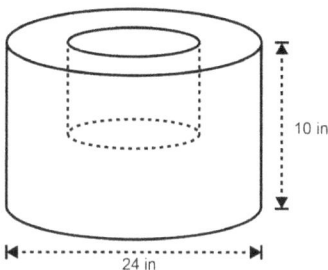

**Note:** Figure not drawn to scale

**2. What is the volume of the above solid made by a hollow cylinder that is half the size (in all dimensions) of the larger cylinder?**

   a. 1440 π in³
   b. 1260 π in³
   c. 1040 π in³
   d. 960 π in³

**3. Tony bought 15 dozen eggs for $80. 16 eggs were broken during loading and unloading. He sold the remaining eggs for $0.54 each. What will be his percent profit?**

   a. 11%
   b. 10%
   c. 13%
   d. 12%

**4. In a class of 83 students, 72 are present. What percent of students are absent?**

   a. 12%
   b. 13%
   c. 14%
   d. 15%

# TABE® SKILL PRACTICE

**5.** A student deposits $200 in a savings account hoping to buy a bicycle worth $245. If the bank offers a 15% interest rate, how long will she have to wait?

    a. 1½ years

    b. 2 ½ years

    c. 2 years

    d. 1 year

**6.** A man earns $600 as interest after 2 years of depositing a certain amount in a local bank. If the interest rate was 3%, how much was the original amount deposited?

    a. $3,600

    b. $100,000

    c. $10,000

    d. $1,000

**Consider the following graph.**

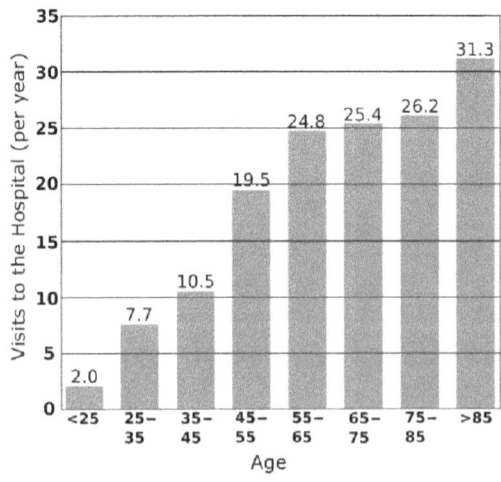

**7. How many hospital visits per year does a person aged 85 or older make?**

   a. 26.2

   b. 31.3

   c. More than 31.3

   d. A decision cannot be made from this graph.

**8. Based on this graph, how many visits per year do you expect a person that is 95 or older to make?**

   a. More than 31.3

   b. Less than 31.3

   c. 31.3

   d. A decision cannot be made from this graph.

**9. How much water can be stored in a cylindrical container 5 meters in diameter and 12 meters high?**

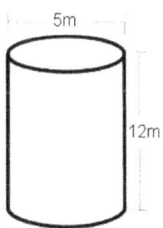

**Note:** Figure not drawn to scale

   a. 235.65 m³

   b. 223.65 m³

   c. 240.65 m³

   d. 252.65 m³

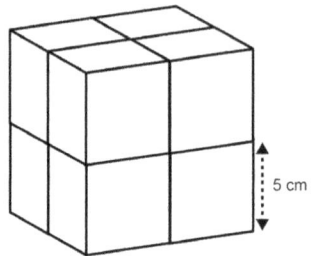

**Note:** Figure not drawn to scale

**10. Assuming the figure is composed of cubes, what is the volume of the figure above?**

    a. 125 cm³

    b. 875 cm³

    c. 1000 cm³

    d. 500 cm³

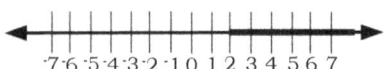

**11. Choose the expression the figure represents.**

    a. X > 2

    b. X ≥ 2

    c. X < 2

    d. X ≤ 2

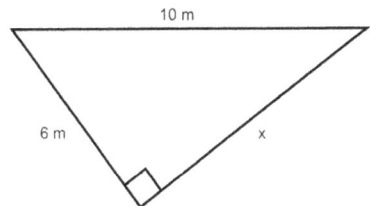

**12. What is the length of the missing side in the triangle above?**

    a. 6
    b. 4
    c. 8
    d. 5

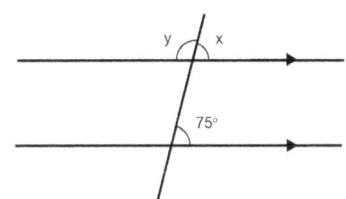

**13. What is the value of the angle y?**

    a. 25°
    b. 15°
    c. 30°
    d. 105°

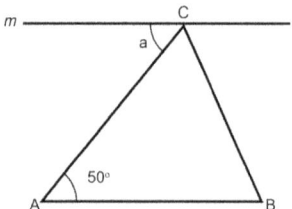

**14. If the line *m* is parallel to the side AB of △ABC, what is angle *a*?**

    a. 130°
    b. 25°
    c. 65°
    d. 50°

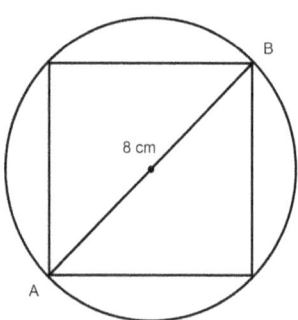

**Note:** Figure not drawn to scale

**15. What is area of the circle?**

    a. 4 π cm²
    b. 12 π cm²
    c. 10 π cm²
    d. 16 π cm²

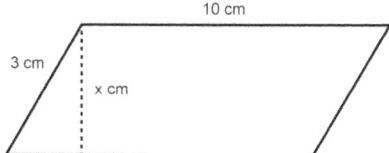

**16. What is the perimeter of the parallelogram above?**

    a. 12 cm
    b. 26 cm
    c. 13 cm
    d. (13+x) cm

**17. Express 87% as a decimal.**

    a. .087
    b. 8.7
    c. .87
    d. 87

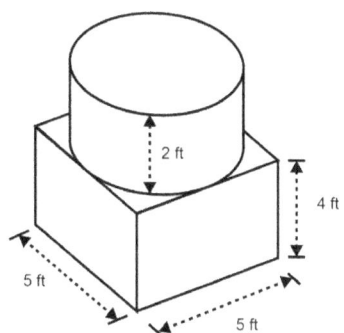

**Note:** Figure not drawn to scale

**18. What is the approximate total volume of the above solid?**

    a. 120 ft³

    b. 100 ft³

    c. 140 ft³

    d. 160 ft³

**19. Susan wants to buy a leather jacket that costs $545.00 and is on sale for 10% off. What is the approximate cost?**

    a. $525

    b. $450

    c. $475

    d. $500

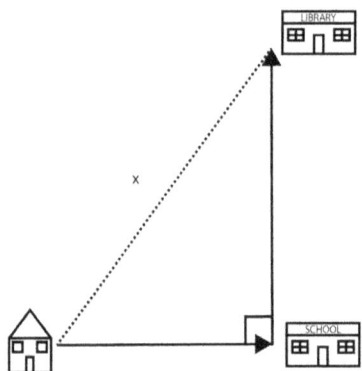

Note: Figure not drawn to scale

**20. Every day starting from his home Peter travels due east 3 kilometers to the school. After school he travels due north 4 kilometers to the library. What is the distance between Peter's home and the library?**

    a. 15 km

    b. 10 km

    c. 5 km

    d. 12 ½ km

# PRACTICE TEST QUESTIONS 2     109

**21. If Tim deposits $5,500 in a savings account that offers a 5% interest, what will be the total amount in his savings account after 3 years?**

    a. $6,225

    b. $6,0325

    c. $325

    d. $6,325

**22. The cost of waterproofing canvas is .50 per square yard. What is the total cost for waterproofing a canvas truck cover that is 15' x 24'?**

    a. $18.00

    b. $6.67

    c. $180.00

    d. $20.00

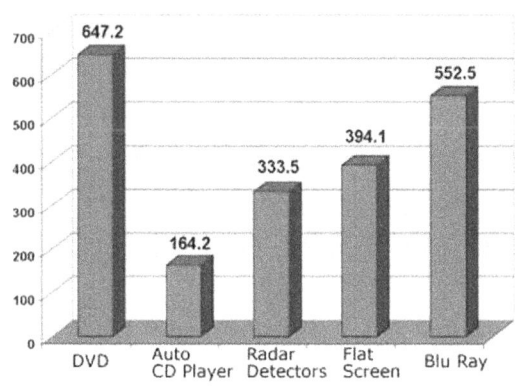

**23. Consider the graph above. What is the third best-selling product?**

    a. Radar Detectors

    b. Flat Screen TV

    c. Blu Ray

    d. Auto CD Players

**24. Which two products are the closest in the number of sales?**

    a. Blu Ray and Flat Screen TV
    b. Flat Screen TV and Radar Detectors
    c. Radar Detectors and Auto CD Players
    d. DVD players and Blu Ray

**25. A small business owner deposits $6000 in a savings account at a local bank. After 2 years, at 3% interest rate, what will be the interest earned?**

    a. $6360
    b. $360
    c. $240
    d. $460

# Language

Directions: Fill in the blank with the correct punctuation.

**1. The recipe requires the following ingredients \_\_\_\_ flour, sugar, eggs, baking powder and vanilla.**

    a. ,
    b. :
    c. ;
    d. .

**2. Lindsay said \_\_\_\_ "It's a beautiful day."**

    a. ,
    b. :
    c. ;
    d. .

## Practice Test Questions 2

3. Dear Ms. Smith___

    a. :
    b. ,
    c. .
    d. !

4. Her sister___s bag was full of useless items

    a. " "
    b. '
    c. ,
    d. –

5. Actors try to empathize with ___to share the feelings of ___ the characters they portray.

    a. ( )
    b. { }
    c. [ ]
    d. " "

6. Choose the sentence below with the correct punctuation.

    a. Puzzled — Joe said, "You aren't going to pay me until ?"
    b. Puzzled, Joe said, "You aren't going to pay me until ?"
    c. Puzzled, Joe said, "You aren't going to pay me until —?"
    d. Puzzled, Joe said, "You aren't going to pay me until, ?"

7. Choose the sentence below with the correct punctuation.

   a. His employment wasn't consecutive, from 1999 to 2001 and 2002 – 2004.

   b. His employment wasn't consecutive, from 1999 – 2001 and 2002 – 2004.

   c. His employment wasn't consecutive, from 1999 _ 2001    and 2002_ 2004.

   d. His employment wasn't consecutive, from 1999, 2001 and 2002, 2004.

8. Choose the sentence below with the correct punctuation.

   a. Sandy asked for a one/third reduction on the cost of her damaged bag.

   b. Sandy asked for a one, third reduction on the cost of her damaged bag.

   c. Sandy asked for a one-third reduction on the cost of her damaged bag.

   d. None of the Above.

9. Choose the sentence below with the correct punctuation.

   a. Three minutes, two minutes, one minute

   b. Three minutes ... two minutes ... one minutes

   c. Three minutes - two minutes - one minutes

   d. None of the Above.

# Practice Test Questions 2

**10. Choose the sentence below with the correct punctuation.**

a. Ms. Hermandez has offered to coach the basketball team, however, the competition is intense.

b. Ms. Hermandez has offered to coach the basketball team, however the competition is intense.

c. Ms. Hermandez has offered to coach the team; however, the competition is intense.

d. None of the Above.

**Directions: for questions 5 - 10 choose the sentence with the correct punctuation and capitalization.**

**11. Choose the sentence with the correct punctuation and capitalization.**

a. The teacher just told us that it's time for the test.

b. Although his' car was fairly new he sold it to the banker.

c. She moved out of her parents' house into her's.

d. Who's brand new Camaro is this parked on the lawn?

**12. Choose the sentence with the correct punctuation and capitalization.**

a. I went to the supermarket: I bought chicken rice and fruits.

b. Iv'e never been this much in love before: until you.

c. I've just eaten these fruits; apples, peaches, plums and grapes.

d. The worst vices are: prostitution, gambling and drug trafficking.

**13. Choose the sentence with the correct punctuation and capitalization.**

a. The writer J. K. Rowling is British.

b. Have you seen my best Friend Scott who lives next door?

c. J. R. R. Tolkien, wrote the Lord of the Rings.

d. The US president, Barak Obama, arrived yesterday.

**14. Choose the sentence with the correct punctuation and capitalization.**

a. This video game is not interesting said Bobby to his friend.

b. This Video game is not interesting, said Bobby, to his friend.

c. "This video game is not interesting." Said Bobby to his friend.

d. "This video game is not interesting," said Bobby to his friend.

**15. Choose the sentence with the correct punctuation and capitalization.**

a. James Smith, the president of the club, invited the members to a party.

b. The president of the club James Smith, invited the members to a party.

c. The president of the club James Smith invited the members to a party.

d. James Smith the president of the club invited the members to a party.

**16. Combine the following two sentences into one sentence with the same meaning.**

**Lisa applies herself to her studies.**
**Lisa may achieve excellent grades.**

   a. Lisa may achieve excellent grades to apply herself to her studies.

   b. If Lisa achieves good grades she may apply herself to her studies.

   c. Lisa applies herself to her studies although she may achieve excellent grades.

   d. Lisa may achieve excellent grades once she applies herself to her studies.

**17. Combine the following two sentences into one sentence with the same meaning.**

**Richard took lessons in Spanish.**
**Richard wanted a job at the Spanish Embassy.**

   a. Richard took lessons in Spanish so that he wanted a job at the Spanish Embassy.

   b. Richard took lessons in Spanish since he wanted a job at the Spanish Embassy.

   c. Even if Richard wanted a job at the Spanish Embassy he took lessons in Spanish.

   d. Having taken a job at the Spanish Embassy, Richard took lessons in Spanish.

**18. Combine the following two sentences into one sentence with the same meaning.**

**The principal gives Bob a warning.**
**Bob does not disobey the rules.**

   a. If the principal gives Bob a warning he does not disobey the rules.

   b. Bob does not disobey the rules but also the principal gives him a warning

   c. Even if the principal gives Bob a warning he does not disobey the rules.

   d. The principal gives Bob a warning so that he does not disobey the rules.


**19. Combine the following two sentences into one sentence with the same meaning.**

**Linda was very late for school.**
**Linda missed an important subject.**

   a. Because Linda missed an important subject she was very late for school.

   b. Linda missed an important subject so that she was late for school.

   c. Linda was so late for school that she missed an important subject.

   d. Although Linda was very late for school, she missed an important subject.

# Practice Test Questions 2

**20. Combine the following two sentences into one sentence with the same meaning.**

**Mary worked hard.**

**Mary succeeded at her job.**

    a. Mary succeeded at her job but she worked hard.

    b. Whenever Mary succeeded at her job she worked hard.

    c. Mary worked hard and thus she succeeded at her job.

    d. However hard Mary worked, she succeeded at her job.

**Directions: For questions 21 - 24 below, you are given a topic sentence. Choose the sentence which best develops the given topic sentence.**

**21. Education is the pathway out of poverty.**

    a. Getting a college education is very expensive.

    b. Over a billion people worldwide earn less than a dollar a day.

    c. Many children in poor countries do not have access to a good education.

    d. Having a college degree results in more earning potential.

**22. Parents should ensure their children's safety near water bodies.**

    a. Families should take trips to the beach together.

    b. CPR is one of the most basic first aid skills.

    c. Young children shouldn't be alone near water.

    d. The earth is divided into four major oceans.

**23. Couples should be properly prepared before having children.**

a. China restricts the number of children a couple may have.

b. There are thousands of children in state care.

c. No contraceptive method is 100 percent safe.

d. The financial and emotional burden must be considered.

**24. The TOEFL test is an adequate assessment of English proficiency.**

a. Nonnative speakers usually find English difficult to learn.

b. English is one of the most widely spoken world languages.

c. American universities require non-natives to pass the TOEFL.

d. The four skill areas are assessed using varied methodology.

**25. A college degree is an essential requirement for a well-paying job.**

a. US and UK colleges are among the best in the world.

b. Some persons complain that their salaries are inadequate.

c. A high-school diploma only gives access to entry-level jobs.

d. Many foreign universities offer scholarships to Americans.

# Practice Test Questions 2

**Questions 26 - 30 refer to the following passage.**

Man has been observing the natural environment for ages and has been using principles learned to advance and improve on various types of technology. <u>The development of gliders is one</u> (26) example. The evolution of gliders originated from man's fascination with bird flight. Gliders were developed after careful study of the flight pattern of birds. The first efforts to duplicate bird-like flying behavior happened from in the early 1800s. <u>In Britain, Sir George Cayley, studying birds, in flight</u> (27), attempted to understand the patterns observed and used the area of mathematics to formulate his observations. He was one first person to formulate mathematical theories about flying. He theorized that the wings, when set at particular angles, caused the bird <u>to ascend glide, or descend</u> (28). From his observations and theories he designed a type of glider and tested its ability to remain in flight, successfully so.

In later years experimenters would come up with their own theories based on their observations and calculations. <u>One sea captain, Jean Marie LeBris, kill an albatross</u> (29) to study its wings and then designed and successfully flew what was later called the LeBris glider in 1857. A German, Otto Lilienthal, went even further. He covered peeled willow wands with waxed cotton cloth in his glider design. This design made several thousand flights, with constant improvements. The art of making gliders <u>has been perfected</u> (30) over the years. Gliders nowadays are able to fly for hundreds of miles.

**Read the passage below and look at the numbered, underlined phrases. Choose the answer that is written correctly for each underlined part.**

**26. Choose the correct version.**

    a. The development of Gliders is one

    b. The development of gliders are one

    c. The development of gliders is some

    d. Correct as is.

**27. Choose the correct version.**

a. In Britain, Sir George Cayley, studying birds in flight
b. In Britain; Sir George Cayley studying birds in flight
c. In Britain Sir George Cayley, studying birds in flight
d. Correct as is.

**28. Choose the correct version.**

a. to ascend glide or descend
b. to ascend, glide or descend
c. to ascend, glide nor descend
d. Correct as is.

**29. Choose the correct version.**

a. One sea captain, Jean Marie LeBris, killed an albatross
b. One sea captain – Jean Marie LeBris; kill an albatross
c. One sea captain: Jean Marie LeBris: kills an albatross
d. Correct as is.

**30. Choose the correct version.**

a. have been perfected
b. was been perfected
c. has being perfected
d. Correct as is.

## Vocabulary

31. Because of its colorful fall _____, the maple is my favorite tree.

    a. Growth
    b. Branches
    c. Greenery
    d. Foliage

32. When Mr. Davis returned from southern Asia, he told us about the _____ that sometimes swept the area, bringing torrential rain.

    a. Monsoons
    b. Hurricanes
    c. Blizzards
    d. Floods

33. In heavily industrialized areas, the pollution of the air causes many to develop _____ diseases.

    a. Respiratory
    b. Cardiac
    c. Alimentary
    d. Circulatory

34. You can _____ some fires by covering them with dirt, while others require foam or water.

    a. Extinguish
    b. Distinguish
    c. Ignite
    d. Lessen

**35.** Through the use of powerful fans that circulate the heat over the food, _____ ovens work very efficiently.

    a. Microwave
    b. Broiler
    c. Convection
    d. Pressure

**For questions 36 - 40, choose the word that best completes both sentences.**

**36.** She always _____ people behind their back.
He _____ his opponents in his speeches.

    a. Offends
    b. Belittle
    c. Avoid
    d. Admire

**37.** They aren't exciting - all of the pictures are very _____.
His clothes are always very _____.

    a. Exciting
    b. Continuous
    c. Unforgiving
    d. Mundane

**38.** The auditorium was _____ when we arrived.
With 8 children, their house is always _____.

    a. Bedlam
    b. Placid
    c. Calm
    d. Noise

## Practice Test Questions 2

39. I would like to _____ if possible.
They tried, but couldn't _____ the disaster.

    a. Avert

    b. Promote

    c. Avenge

    d. Facilitate

40. The water will soon _____.
It is all gone. The water _____ over the last hour.

    a. Drip

    b. Dissipate

    c. Appear

    d. Degenerate

# 124 TABE® SKILL PRACTICE

## Answer Key

## Reading

**1. A**
Choice B is incorrect; the author did not express their opinion on the subject matter. Choice C is incorrect, the author was not trying to prove a point, nor is the author trying to persuade.

**2. C**
Choice C is correct; historians believe it was brutal and bloody. Choice A is incorrect; there is no consensus that the Crusades achieved great things. Choice B is incorrect; it did not stabilize the Holy Lands. Choice D is incorrect, some historians do believe this was the purpose but not all historians.

**3. D**
The feudal system led to infighting. Choice A is incorrect, it had the opposite effect. Choice B is incorrect, though this is a good answer, it is not the best answer. The Church asked for volunteers not the Feudal Lords. Choice C is incorrect, it did have an effect on the Crusades.

**4. A**
Saracen was a generic term for Muslims widely used in Europe during the later medieval era.

**5. B**
This warranty does not cover a product that you have tried to fix yourself. From paragraph two, "This limited warranty does not cover ... any unauthorized disassembly, repair, or modification. "

**6. C**
ABC Electric could either replace or repair the fan, provided the other conditions are met. ABC Electric has the option to repair or replace.

**7. B**
The warranty does not cover a stove damaged in a flood.

From the passage, "This limited warranty does not cover any damage to the product from improper installation, accident, abuse, misuse, natural disaster, insufficient or excessive electrical supply, abnormal mechanical or environmental conditions."

A flood is an "abnormal environmental condition," and a natural disaster, so it is not covered.

**8. A**
A missing part is an example of defective workmanship. This is an error made in the manufacturing process. A defective part is not considered workmanship.

**9. D**
This question tests the reader's summarization skills. The other choices A, B, and C focus on portions of the second paragraph that are too narrow and do not relate to the specific portion of text in question. The complexity of the sentence may mislead students into selecting one of these answers, but rearranging or restating the sentence will lead the reader to the correct answer. In addition, choice A makes an assumption that may or may not be true about the intentions of the company, choice B focuses on one product rather than the idea of the products, and choice C makes an assumption about women that may or may not be true and is not supported by the text.

**10. B**
This question tests reader's attention to detail. If a reader selects A, he or she may have picked up on the use of the word "debate" and assumed, very logically, that the two are at odds because they are fighting; however, this is simply not supported in the text. Choice C also uses very specific quotes from the text, but it rearranges and gives them false meaning. The artists want to elevate their creations above the creations of other artists, thereby showing that they are "creative" and "innovative." Similarly, choice D takes phrases straight from the text and rearranges and confuses them. The artists are described as wanting to be "creative, innovative, individual people," not the women.

## 11. A

This question tests reader's vocabulary and summarization skills. This phrase, used by the author, may seem flippant and dismissive if readers focus on the word "whatever" and misinterpret it as a popular, colloquial term. In this way, Choices B and C may mislead the reader to selecting one of them by including the terms "unimportant" and "stupid," respectively. Choice D is a similar misreading, but doesn't make sense when the phrase is at the beginning of the passage and the entire passage is on media messages. Choice A is literally and contextually appropriate, and the reader can understand that the author would like to keep the introduction focused on the topic the passage is going to discuss.

## 12. A

This question tests a reader's inference skills. The extreme use of the word "all" in choice B suggests that every single advertising company are working to be approachable, and while this is not only unlikely, the text specifically states that "more" companies have done this, signifying that they have not all participated, even if it's a possibility that they may some day. The use of the limiting word "only" in choice C lends that answer similar problems; women are still buying from companies who do not care about this message, or those companies would not be in business, and the passage specifies that "many" women are worried about media messages, but not all. Readers may find choice D logical, especially if they are looking to make an inference, and while this may be a possibility, the passage does not suggest or discuss this happening. Choice A is correct based on specifically because of the relation between "still working" in the answer and "will hopefully" and the extensive discussion on companies struggles, which come only with progress, in the text.

## 13. C

This question tests the reader's summarization skills. The entire passage is leading up to the idea that the president of the US may not have had grounds to assert his Fourteen Points when other countries had lost so much. Choice A is pretty directly inferred by the text, but it does not adequately summarize what the entire passage is trying to communicate. Choice B may also be inferred by the passage when it says that the war is "imminent," but it does not represent the entire message, either. The passage does seem to be in praise of FDR, or at least in respect of him, but it does not in any way claim that he is the smartest president, nor does this represent the many other points included. Choice C is then the obvious answer, and most directly relates to the closing sentences which it rewords.

**14. C**
This question tests the reader's attention to detail. The passage does state that choices A and B are true, and while those statements are in proximity to the explanation for why the war started, they are not the reason given. Choice D is a mix up of words used in the passage, which says that the largest powers were in play but not that this fact somehow started the war. The passage does make a direct statement that a domino effect started the war, supporting choice C as the correct answer.

**15. A**
This question tests the reader's understanding of functions in writing. Throughout the passage, it states that leaders of other nations were hesitant to accept generous or peaceful terms because of the grievances of the war, and the great loss of life was chief among these. While the passage does touch on the devastation of deadly weapons (B), the use of this raw, emotional fact serves a larger purpose, and the focus of the passage is not weapons. While readers may indeed consider who lost the most soldiers (C) when, so many countries were involved and the inequalities of loss are mentioned in the passage, there is no discussion of this in the passage. Choice D is related to A, but choice A is more direct and relates more to the passage.

**16. B**
This question tests the reader's vocabulary skills. Choice A may seem appealing to readers because it is phonetically similar to "catalyzed," but the two are not related in any other way. Choice C makes sense in context, but if plugged in to the sentence creates a redundancy that doesn't make sense. Choice D does also not make sense contextually, even if the reader may consider that funds were needed to create more weaponry, especially if it was advanced.

# TABE® SKILL PRACTICE

**17. A**
Victoria is about 5 miles from Burnaby.

**18. B**
The Village Hall is about 5 miles from Victoria.

**19. A**
The correct order of ingredients is brown sugar, baking soda and chocolate chips.

**20. B**
Sturdy: strong, solid in structure or person. In context, Stir in chocolate chips by hand with a *sturdy* wooden spoon.

**21. A**
Disperse: to scatter in different directions or break up. In context, Stir until the chocolate chips and nuts are evenly *dispersed*.

**22. B**
You can stop stirring the nuts when they are evenly distributed. From the passage, "Stir until the chocolate chips and nuts are evenly dispersed."

**23. B**
Choice A is incorrect as the Monster killed Frankenstein, not the other way around. Choice B is correct, Frankenstein is dead. Choice C is incorrect - Mary Shelley is the author. Choice D is incorrect, the person is called Frankenstein.

**24. C**
The speaker 'suspended' from following through on his duty to destroy the monster due to curiosity and compassion. The other choices may seem reasonable, but are not explicitly given in the passage.

**25. D**
All the choices are correct. Frankenstein's monster destroys Frankenstein by

   a. By killing Frankenstein

   b. By letting himself be the monster everyone sees him as

   c. By destroying everything Frankenstein loved

# Practice Test Questions 2

## Computational Mathematics

**1. C**
8974 − 8256 = 718

**2. A**
4404 / 8 = 550.5

**3. D**
274 * 139 = 38086

**4. B**
3567 + 99 = 3666

**5. A**
2 + a number divided by 7.
(2 + X) divided by 7.
(2 + X)/7

**6. A**
60/x = 75/100
60 * 100/X = 75
6000/75 = X
X = 80

**7. C**
71 ÷ 1000 = 0.071.

**8. A**
.33 × .59 = .195

**9. A**
Collect like terms, 7x = 47 + 9 = 56,
divide both sides by 7
x = 8

**10. C**
The ten thousandths place in 1.7389 will be the 4$^{th}$ decimal place, 9.

**11. A**
.87 - .48 = 0.39.

**12. C**
Forty nine thousandths will place the '9' in the 3rd decimal place, 0.049.

**13. C**
a. 3/4 * 2/2 = 6/8
b. 3/4 * 3/3 = 9/12
c. 3/4 * 4/4 = 12/16 - Incorrect
d. 3/4 * 7/7 = 21/28

**14. D**
a. 84/231 = 12/33 > 1/3
b. 6/35 = 1/5 < 1/3
c. 3/22 = 1/7 < 1/3
d. b and c are less than 1/3

**15. C**
Here are the choices:
a. 1
b. √2 = 1.414
c. 3/2 = 1.5   Largest number
d. 4/3 = 1.33

**16. B**
Collecting similar terms (algebraic addition).
2b + 9b – 5b = 11b - 5b = 6b

**17. C**
4.7 + .9 + .01 = 5.61.

**18. D**
60/100 = 12/X
60 = 12 * 100/X
60X = 1200
X = 1200/60
X = 20.

**19. D**
.84/.7 = 1.2

**20. C**
4120 – 3216 = 904

**21. D**
2417 + 1004 = 3421

# Practice Test Questions 2

**22. B**
0.12 + 2/5 - 3/5, Convert decimal to fraction to get 3/25 + 2/5 - 3/5, = (3 + 10)/25 - 15/25, = - 2/25.

**23. D**
700,653 – 70,099 = 630,554

**24. A**
0.25 + 2 1/3 + 2/3, first convert decimal to fraction, 1/4 + 1/3 + 2/3, (3 + 4 + 8)/12, = 15/12 = 5/4 = 1 1/4

**25. B**
10% of 300 = 30 and 50% of 20 = 10 so 30 + 10 = 40.

# Applied Mathematics

**1. C**
1 hour is equal to 3,600 seconds and 1 kilometer is equal to 1000 meters.

Since this train travels 72 kilometers per hour, this means that it covers 72,000 meters in 3,600 seconds.

If it travels 72,000 meters in 3,600 seconds

It travels x meters in 12 seconds

By cross multiplication: x = 72,000 • 12 / 3,600

x = 240 meters

**2. B**
Total Volume = Volume of large cylinder - Volume of small cylinder

Volume of a cylinder = area of base • height = $\pi r^2 \cdot h$

Total Volume = ($\pi$ * 12² * 10) - ($\pi$ * 6² * 5) = 1440$\pi$ - 180$\pi$

= 1260$\pi$ in³

**3. A**
Let us first mention the money Tony spent: $80

Now we need to find the money Tony earned:

He had 15 dozen eggs = 15 * 12 = 180 eggs. 16 eggs were

broken. So,

Remaining number of eggs that Tony sold = 180 − 16 = 164.

Total amount he earned for selling 164 eggs = 164 * 0.54 = $88.56.

As a summary, he spent $80 and earned $88.56.

The profit is the difference: 88.56 - 80 = $8.56

Percentage profit is found by proportioning the profit to the money he spent:

8.56•100/80 = 10.7%

Checking the answers, we round 10.7 to the nearest whole number: 11%

**4. B**
Number of absent students = 83 − 72 = 11

Percentage of absent students is found by proportioning the number of absent students to total number of students in the class = (11 * 100)/83 = 13.25

Checking the answers, we round 13.25 to the nearest whole number: 13%

**5. A**
P = 200, r = 15%, I = 245 − 200 = $45, t =? First convert the rate to a decimal, 15% = 0.15. I = P x r x t. Therefore, 45 = 200 x 0.15 x t, 45 = 30t, t = 45/30 = 1.5. She will have to wait for 1½ years for his $200 to earn $45 interest to become $245.

**6. C**
I = 600, r = 3, t = 2 and P = ? Using the formula, P = 100 x interest/ r x t

100 x 600/ 3 x 2 = 60000/6 = 10,000. The original amount deposited was $10,000

**7. B**
Based on this graph, a person that is 85 or older will make 31.3 visits to the hospital every year.

# Practice Test Questions 2     133

**8. A**
Based on this graph, the number of visits per year is going up as age goes up, so we can expect a person that is 95 to have more than 31.3 visits to the hospital each year.

**9. A**
The formula of the volume of cylinder is the base area multiplied by the height. As the formula:

Volume of a cylinder = $\pi r^2 h$. Where $\pi$ is 3.142, r is radius of the cross sectional area, and h is the height.

We know that the diameter is 5 meters, so the radius is 5/2 = 2.5 meters.

The volume is: V = 3.142 * 2.5² * 12 = 235.65 m³.

**10. C**
The large cube is made up of 8 smaller cubes with 5 cm sides. The volume of a cube is found by the third power of the length of one side.
Volume of the large cube = Volume of the small cube•8

= $(5^3)$•8 = 125•8

= 1000 cm³

There is another solution for this question. Find the side length of the large cube. There are two cubes rows with 5 cm length for each. So, one side of the large cube is 10 cm.

The volume of this large cube is equal to $10^3$ = 1000 cm³

**11. A**
The line is pointing towards numbers greater than 2. The equation is therefore, X > 2.

**12. C**
**Pythagorean Theorem:**
(Hypotenuse)² = (Perpendicular)² + (Base)²
$h^2 = a^2 + b^2$

Given: a = 6, h = 10
$h^2 = a^2 + b^2$
$b^2 = h^2 - a^2$

$b^2 = 10^2 + 6^2$
$b^2 = 100 - 36$
$b^2 = 64$
$b = 8$

## 13. D

As shown in the figure, two parallel lines intersecting with a third line with angle of 75°.

$x = 75°$ (corresponding angles)

$x + y = 180°$ (supplementary angles) ... inserting the value of x here:

$y = 180° - 75°$
$y = 105°$

## 14. D

Two parallel lines (m & side AB) intersected by side AC. This means that 50° and a angles are interior angles. So:
$a = 50°$ (interior angles).

## 15. D

We have a circle given with diameter 8 cm and a square located within the circle. We are asked to find the area of the circle for which we only need to know the length of the radius that is the half of the diameter.
Area of circle = $\pi r^2$ ... r = 8/2 = 4 cm

Area of circle = $\pi \cdot 4^2$

= $16\pi$ cm² ... As we notice, the inner square has no role in this question.

## 16. B

Perimeter of a parallelogram is the sum of the sides.
Perimeter = 2(l + b)
Perimeter = 2(3 + 10), 2 x 13
Perimeter = 26 cm.

## 17. C

87% = 87/100 = 0.87

## PRACTICE TEST QUESTIONS 2

**18. C**
Volume of a cylinder is π x r² x h
Diameter = 5 ft. so radius is 2.5 ft.
Volume of cylinder= π x 2.5² x 2
= π x 6.25 x 2 = 12.5 π
Approximate π to 3.142
Volume of the cylinder = 39.25

Volume of a rectangle = height X width X length.
= 5 X 5 X 4 = 100

Total volume = Volume of rectangular solid + volume of cylinder
Total volume = 100 + 39.25
Total volume = 139.25 ft³ or about 140 ft³

**19. D**
The jacket costs $545.00 so we can round up to $550. 10% of $550 is 55. We can round down to $50, which is easier to work with. $550 - $50 is $500. The jacket will cost about $500.

The actual cost will be 10% X 545 = $54.50
545 − 54.50 = $490.50

**20. C**
We see that two legs of a right triangle form by Peter's movements and we are asked to find the length of the hypotenuse. We use the Pythagorean Theorem:

(Hypotenuse)² = (Perpendicular)² + (Base)²
h² = a² + b²

Given: 3² + 4² = h²
h² = √25
h = 5

**21. D**
P= $5,500, t = 3 years, r = 5%, I = ? convert rate to decimal and 5% = 0.05
I = 5,500 x 0.05 x 3 = 825. Total amount in the account = principal + interest or 5,500 + 825 = $6,325

### 22. D
First calculate total square feet, which is 15 * 24 = 360 ft². Next, convert this value to square yards, (1 yards² = 9 ft²) which is 360/9 = 40 yards². At $0.50 per square yard, the total cost is 40 * 0.50 = $20.

### 23. B
Flat Screen TVs are the third best-selling product.

### 24. B
The two products that are closest in the number of sales, are Flat Screen TVs and Radar Detectors.

### 25. B
I = ?, r = 3%, t = 2 years, P = 6000. Convert rate to decimal. 3% = 0.03. Then plug in variables into the simple interest formula. I = P x r x t, I = 6000 x 0.03 x 2, I = $360.

# Language

### 1. B
A colon is used before a list of items following an independent clause.

### 2. A
A comma is used to introduce short quotations or proverbs.

### 3. A
The colon is used in the salutation of a formal business letter.

### 4. B
An apostrophe is placed before the letter "s" to indicate singular possession.

### 5. A
A parenthesis is used to set off asides and explanations only when the material is not essential or when it consists of one or more sentences.

### 6. C
The dash is used when the speaker cannot continue.

# Practice Test Questions 2

**7. B**
The dash is used to show a closed range of values.

**8. C**
A hyphen is used with fractions used as adjectives.

**9. B**
Ellipsis (…) is used to indicate passage of time.

**10. A**
"However" generally has a comma before and after.

**11. A**
Choice A uses the apostrophe correctly in "it's." All the other choices have incorrect apostrophe use.

**12. A**
Choice A uses the colon correctly. Choice B uses the incorrect form, "Iv'e." Choice C uses a semicolon instead of a colon. Choice D uses the colon incorrectly.

**13. A**
Choice A has correct punctuation and capitalization. Choice B incorrectly capitalizes "friend." Choice C uses a comma incorrectly. In choice D, "president" should be capitalized.

**14. D**
Choice A is incorrect because it does not use quotation marks. Choice B does not use quotation marks and incorrectly places a comma after Bobby. Choice C incorrectly places a period after Bobby.

**15. A**
Choice A is the only choice which uses the comma correctly.

**16. D**
**17. B**
**18. D**
**19. C**
**20. C**
**21. D**
**22. C**
**23. D**

**24. D**

**25. C**

**26. D**
The phrase is correct as is. Choice A incorrectly capitalizes "gliders." Choice B incorrectly uses "are." Choice C incorrectly uses "some."

**27. A**
Choice A uses commas correctly. Choice B incorrectly uses a semi colon instead of a comma. Choice C omits a comma after "Britain."

**28. B**
Choice B is the only choice that uses commas correctly.

**29. A**
Choice A uses commas correctly. Choice B uses the dash where it is not needed, and a semi colon instead of a comma. Choice C uses colons instead of comma.

**30. D**
The phrase is correct as is, and uses the past perfect correctly. The other choices all use the past perfect incorrectly.

## Vocabulary

**31. D**
**Foliage:** plant leaves

**32. A**
**Monsoons:** a seasonal prevailing wind in the region of South and Southeast Asia, blowing from the southwest between May and September and bringing rain

**33. A**
**Respiratory:** of, relating to, or affecting respiration or the organs of respiration.

**34. A**
**Extinguish:** cause (a fire or light) to cease to burn or shine.

**35. C**
**Convection:** the movement caused within a fluid by the tendency of hotter and therefore less dense material to rise, and colder, denser material to sink under the influence of gravity, which consequently results in transfer of heat.

**36. B**
**Belittle:** make (someone or something) seem unimportant.

**37. D**
**Mundane:** Ordinary; not new.

**38. A**
**Bedlam:** A place or situation of chaotic uproar, and where confusion prevails.

**39. A**
**Avert:** To ward off, or prevent, the occurrence or effects of.

**40. B**
**Dissipate:** disperse or scatter.

# Conclusion

CONGRATULATIONS! You have made it this far because you have applied yourself diligently to practicing for the exam and no doubt improved your potential score considerably! Getting into a good school is a huge step in a journey that might be challenging at times but will be many times more rewarding and fulfilling. That is why being prepared is so important.

Study then Practice and then Succeed!

**Good Luck!**

## FREE Ebook Version

Download a FREE Ebook version of the publication!

Suitable for tablets, iPad, iPhone, or any smart phone.

**Go to**
http://tinyurl.com/o3xqnvn

## Register for Free Updates and More Practice Test Questions

Register your purchase at
https://www.test--preparation.ca/register/
for updates, free test tips and more practice test questions.

# Visit us Online

## www.test-preparation.ca

https://www.facebook.com/CompleteTestPreparation/

https://www.youtube.com/user/MrTestPreparation

https://www.instagram.com/completetestpreparation/

https://www.pinterest.ca/brians6634/boards/

www.ingramcontent.com/pod-product-compliance
Lightning Source LLC
LaVergne TN
LVHW010301260326
834688LV00044B/1394